ISBN: 9781290644716


Published by:
HardPress Publishing
8345 NW 66TH ST #2561
MIAMI FL 33166-2626

Email: info@hardpress.net
Web: http://www.hardpress.net

# The Temple Library

# ESSAYS OF LEIGH HUNT

*This edition is limited to Five Hundred copies for England and Five Hundred for America (acquired by* MESSRS. MACMILLAN AND CO.). *There is also an Edition, on large paper, limited to Two Hundred and Twenty-five copies* (150 *for England*).

J. M. DENT AND CO.

Leigh Hunt.

# ESSAYS

## OF

# LEIGH HUNT

## SELECTED AND EDITED

### BY

## REGINALD BRIMLEY JOHNSON

### WITH INTRODUCTION

*PORTRAIT BY S. LAWRENCE*
*AND ETCHINGS BY HERBERT RAILTON*

## LONDON
## J. M. DENT AND CO.
### 69 GREAT EASTERN STREET
### 1891

# VOL. I.

# CONTENTS.

|  | PAGE |
|---|---|
| Preface | ix |
| Introduction | xi |

### ESSAYS, MISCELLANEOUS, CRITICAL, AND AUTOBIOGRAPHICAL.

|  | |
|---|---|
| Deaths of Little Children | 1 |
| Child-Bed | 7 |
| An Earth upon Heaven | 8 |
| Thoughts and Guesses on Human Nature | 15 |
| Angling | 17 |
| February | 23 |
| March | 23 |
| May | 24 |
| Dawn | 24 |
| Fine Days in January and February | 26 |
| The Walk in the Wood | 29 |
| A " Now," Descriptive of a Hot Day | 30 |
| A " Now," Descriptive of a Cold Day | 35 |
| Getting up on Cold Mornings | 42 |
| The Old Gentleman | 49 |
| The Old Lady | 55 |
| The Maid-Servant | 60 |
| The Waiter | 65 |
| Seamen on Shore | 70 |
| Coaches | 80 |
| [From] A Visit to the Zoological Gardens | 108 |

PAGE

A Letter to the Bells of a Parish Church in Italy . 111
The True Enjoyment of Splendour :—A Chinese
    Apologue . . . . . . . . 116
Wit made Easy, or, A Hint to Word-Catchers . . 120
The Prince on St. Patrick's Day . . . . . 125
An Answer to the Question, What is Poetry ? . . 127
Reason in Poetry . . . . . . . . 128
Wit and Humour . . . . . . . . 129
On the Representation of Tragedy . . . . 132
Table Talk . . . . . . . . . 135
Spenser . . . . . . . . . . 136
Shakespeare . . . . . . . . . 137
Beaumont and Fletcher . . . . . . 140
Samuel Butler . . . . . . . . 143
Pope . . . . . . . . . . 145
An Evening with Pope . . . . . . . 147
Gray . . . . . . . . . . 148
Goldsmith . . . . . . . . . 150
Burns . . . . . . . . . . 151
Wordsworth . . . . . . . . . 152
Coleridge . . . . . . . . . 153
Lamb . . . . . . . . . . 157
Shelley . . . . . . . . . . 161
The Colman Family . . . . . . . 171
John Buncle . . . . . . . . . 178
My Books . . . . . . . . . 181
Dedication to " Foliage," 1818, to Sir John Edward
    Swinburne, Bart. . . . . . . . 206
A Schoolboy's First Love . . . . . . 207
An Account of Christ-Hospital . . . . . 211
His Jailers . . . . . . . . . 224
Maiano . . . . . . . . . . 229
The Religion of a Lover of a Truth . . . . 233
Alive . . . . . . . . . . 234

# ILLUSTRATIONS.

Portrait (from a Sketch by Samuel Lawrence, in the possession of Mr. W. Leigh Hunt)  .  *frontispiece*

Chapel at Horsemonger Lane Gaol  .  .  *opposite p.* 126

Christ-Hospital (shewing the window beneath which Leigh Hunt slept, as indicated by his grandson)

*opposite p.* 211

# PREFACE.

THE following selections have been printed from the earliest known editions (although the references in the footnotes apply to the latest editions, for convenience of verification) and to each is prefixed a list of all the occasions on which, so far as I have been able to discover, it has formerly appeared. The essays and poems which are given for the first time in this edition have been printed from copies made by Mr. Alexander Ireland from the original manuscripts, and with the permission of Mr. Walter Leigh Hunt, to whom it seems most probable that the copyright belongs. Messrs. Routledge and Sons have kindly allowed me to include "A Coronation Soliloquy" (vol. ii., p. 76). The authorship of "The Walk in a Wood" (vol. i., p. 29), is indirectly proved by a footnote in one of Mrs. Carlyle's letters (vol. i., p. 104).

Every student of Leigh Hunt owes gratitude to Mr. Alexander Ireland for his invaluable "List of the Writings of William Hazlitt and Leigh Hunt," and I have further to express my thanks to him for the very great personal kindness with which he has always been ready to communicate to me the results of his later researches. I am also under great obligations to Mr. Walter Leigh Hunt, the poet's grandson, especially for his assistance with regard to the list of portraits and the illustrations and for kindly allowing a portrait in his possession to be reproduced for the frontispiece.

To Mr. C. W. Reynell, the lifelong friend of Leigh Hunt, I am indebted for some interesting reminiscences, and to Dr. Richard Garnett for his kind answers to my inquiries. My special thanks are due to Mr. F. J. Sebley of Cambridge, who has allowed me the free use of his valuable collection of early editions of Leigh Hunt, and to my sister, Miss Alice Johnson, for the great care with which she has revised the proofs and for numerous suggestions made by her in the course of the work.

R. B. J.

[NOTE.—The abbreviations in the bibliographies prefixed to the selections are :—

C. Kent for *Leigh Hunt as Poet and Essayist,* edited by C. Kent.

A. Symons for *Essays by Leigh Hunt,* edited by A. Symons.

*Canterbury Poets* for the *Poems of Leigh Hunt and Thomas Hood* (in that series).

*Works* (in vol. ii.) for *Poetical Works.*

In other cases the main part of the title is given.]

# INTRODUCTION.

JAMES HENRY LEIGH HUNT was born on the 19th of October, 1784, in what was then the pretty village of Southgate, county Middlesex, "not only in the lap of the nature which he loved, but in the midst of the truly English scenery which he loved beyond all other." It was doubtless this "scene of trees and meadows, of 'greenery' and nestling cottages," that laid the foundation of his love for the simple beauties of nature, and gave him the same affection for the suburbs of London, that literary associations did for her streets.

He states in his "Autobiography" that "a man is but his parents, or some other of his ancestors, drawn out," and prefaces that work with some very charming sketches of his progenitors. "On the mother's side they seemed all sailors and rough subjects, with a mitigation (on the female part) of quakerism; as, on the father's side, they were creoles and claret drinkers, very polite and clerical." His own father, the Rev. Isaac

Hunt, was more polite than prudent. His firm loyalty made it impossible for him to remain in the West Indies, while the width of his sympathies hindered his preferment at home. As his family increased, and he was not in a position to turn his powers of oratory to financial account, he became acquainted with debtors' prisons, and was constantly in dread of arrest. Yet so capable was he "of settling himself to the most tranquil pleasures," that he could always forget his troubles in reading aloud to his wife with the same fine voice that had first won her heart when he spoke the farewell oration on leaving college. "We thus struggled on between quiet and disturbance, between placid readings and frightful knocks at the door, and sickness, and calamity, and hopes, which hardly ever forsook us."

His wife, Mary Shewell, the daughter of a merchant of Philadelphia, had a disposition the exact reverse of his. " I may call myself," writes her son, "in every sense of the word, etymological not excepted, a son of mirth and melancholy." From his mother Leigh Hunt inherited an "ultra-sympathy with the least show of pain and suffering," and a tendency to fits of depression. But it was no less her memory that stimulated him to an uncompromising uprightness of conduct and gave him "the power of making sacrifices for the sake of a principle." He ventures very hesitatingly to question the full wisdom of her training on account of its tendency to encourage sensitiveness, but he adds at once, "how happy shall I be (if I may) to laugh and compare notes with her on the subject in any humble corner of heaven ; to recall to her the filial tenderness with which she was accustomed to speak of the mistakes of one of her own parents, and to think that her grandchildren will be as kind to the memory of their father." She was a woman of much power through her suffering and her love.

Leigh Hunt was nine years younger than any of his brothers, and thus came more under his mother's influence, which was, at any rate for the moment, an unfortunate preparation for the life of a great school. He went to Christ's Hospital, or Christ-Hospital, as he tells us it should be called, in 1792, at the age of eight, and stayed there till he was sixteen. It was a period of some trouble, and, at the same time, of very great enjoyment. The Spartan system and healthy tone of the school probably helped to strengthen his character, but the course of education was far from being complete. Here he first learnt the meaning of the word compromise. Here he began to take up the cause of independence, and practised resistance to tyranny. Here he at once dreaded and delighted in the haunted cloisters. Here he found his inseparable friend, and here, above all, he devoured Cooke's edition of the British Poets; "he bought them over and over again, and used to get up select sets, which disappeared like buttered crumpets ; for he could resist neither giving them away nor possessing them." He seems at this early age to have acquired the habit of keen and kindly observation, which afterwards enabled him to write such delightful character-sketches in the "Indicator" and elsewhere, and the third and fourth chapters of the "Autobiography" contain the most lifelike pictures of the boys, the masters, and his own place in their midst.

When the time for departure was come he wept bitterly, and took individual leave of every person and spot on the establishment. "I had now a vague sense of worldly trouble, and of a great and serious change in my condition."

He had not meanwhile been left entirely to school influences, for he was always welcomed at three houses where he could share the advantages of family life. First that of Mr. West with "the quiet of [the artist's] gallery, the tranquil, intent beauty of the statues;" then that of Mr. Godfrey Thornton in Austin Friars, "where there was cordiality, and there was music, and a family brimful of hospitality and good-nature, and dear Almeria (now Mrs. P———e), who in vain pretends that she has become aged, which is what she never did, shall, would, might, should, or could do'; " and later that of his aunt Mrs. Dayrell, "another paradise in Great Ormond Street," where he fell in love with his cousin Fan, and acquired a "religious idea of keeping a secret," from having been accidentally present at his brother's private marriage with her sister. He was fortunate in his friends throughout life, or rather his beautiful nature always attracted to itself the most congenial companions.

"For some time after he left school, he did nothing but visit his schoolfellows, haunt the book-stalls, and write verses." His proud and injudicious father collected the verses and published them by subscription in 1801, so that among all whom he was likely to meet the boy became famous in his eighteenth year. Shortly after the publication of these poems he was introduced to the family of Mrs. Kent, lodged for some time in her house, and became engaged to her daughter Marianne. During the greater part of their engagement he seems to have continued living at the houses of various friends, and to have tried his hand at several different employments. He was for a short time a clerk with his brother Stephen, an attorney, and was afterwards placed in the War Office by Mr. Addington.

But his habits of complete absorption in the immediate occupation of the moment left him no faculty for noting the lapse of time, and rendered him unfit for official regularity ; while the work of writing for the papers—particularly as a theatrical critic—with which he filled his leisure hours, was far more congenial to his whole turn of mind. In later life, by great exertions, he partially conquered his difficulty in measuring time, but fortunately he did not cease to write.

At the beginning of 1806 he was living with his brother John, who had been apprenticed to Reynell the printer, and after several more or less abortive attempts to establish newspapers the two brothers started in 1808 " The Examiner," the only one of his papers that succeeded, and by means of which the main part of his political work was achieved. By the end of the same year he felt that he could carry on the paper with greater energy and independence if he resigned his work at the War Office ; and in 1809 his prospects were such as to justify his marriage, *a condition into which he would not enter until he could feel secure of a moderate income in the future.*

Leigh Hunt and Marianne Kent were married on July 3rd, 1809, and spent together a life in which there was much sorrow, and yet no little joy, till her death at the beginning of 1857, rather more than two years before his own.

After he had decided to devote himself to the profession of writing, the outward events of his life, with two exceptions, presented but little variety. He continued to edit papers and write books with extraordinary energy and small financial result. His family increased, and he was constantly moving from house to house, though he lived almost always in one of the London suburbs. He wrote with great care, and seldom with any rapidity, and his ignorance of popular taste prevented him from catching the ear of the public, which was, moreover, prejudiced against him by the scurrilous abuse of Blackwood and the "Quarterly," who spared no weapon against the man for whom they had invented the silly nickname of the "Cockney King." He was not suited by nature for the practical control of a newspaper, and his incapacity for business had been fostered by the peculiar system of Christ-Hospital, where he had not learnt arithmetic, and by a certain inherited incapacity for turning his attention to his own interests. Circumstances and character thus combined to fill his life with anxiety, and it would be a great mistake to think that he took his troubles lightly. His moods of depression, however, were relieved by his healthy power of childlike gaiety, and of burying sorrows in a book. "Those who knew him best would picture him to themselves clothed in a dressing-gown, and bending his head over a book or over the desk. At some periods of his life he rose early, in order that he might get to work early; in other periods he rose late, because he sat over the desk very late. For the most part, however, he habitually came down 'too late' to breakfast, and was no sooner seated sideways at the table than he began to read. After breakfast he repaired to his study, where he remained until he went out to take his walk. He sometimes read at dinner, though not always. At some periods of his life he would sleep after dinner; but usually he retired from the table to read. He read at tea-time, and all the evening read or wrote." So writes Thornton Hunt, and he adds that his father's house was noted at some periods of his life and "among a truly selected circle of friends for the tasteful ease of its conversation and recreation," to which the host's own charming manners added attraction.[1] In his later days indeed when he was regarded as a kind of literary patriarch, numbers of enthusiastic persons came to pay him an homage which he certainly

[1] See references to him in Mrs. Ritchie's fascinating "Chapters from some unwritten Memoirs"—Macmillan's Magazine, Feb. 1891; and in Hawthorne's "Our old Home," vol. ii., p. 175.

appreciated. Under such influences Carlyle refers to his conversation as "free, cheery, idly melodious as bird on bough," and to "his fine, chivalrous, gentlemanly carriage, polite, affectionate, respectful (especially to her [1]) and yet so free and natural."

His greatest friend was Shelley, but the "Autobiography" and "Correspondence" bring out also his intimacy with Keats, Hazlitt, the Lambs, and in a lesser degree the Carlyles, Brownings, Thackeray, etc., etc., while from their biographies we may gather interesting impressions of him.

Every one knows "that in an unfortunate moment Charles Dickens conceived the idea of giving a bright life-likeness to one of his most despicable creations by investing him with a certain atmosphere of gay sentiment, and by attributing to him certain tricks of manner which were generally recognized as Hunt's." [2] It was natural that, at the time, ignorant or careless readers should have supposed the moral characters of the real Hunt and the imaginary Skimpole to be much alike; but there can be no excuse for such a supposition to-day. Dickens' own denial of it was obviously cordial and genuine, while our knowledge of Leigh Hunt shows him to have been a man of courageous as well as sensitive morality, and of the strictest integrity. His writings alone afford indisputable testimony to his purity of thought and principle.

The two events to which I have referred, as

[1] Mrs. Carlyle.

[2] From a most interesting article on "Leigh Hunt, his life, character, and work," in the "London Quarterly Review," written, I believe, by Mr. J. A. Noble, author of "The Pelican Papers."

having broken into the regular routine of his daily life, were also its most serious troubles—his imprisonment and his visit to Italy.

Somebody said once that " poor L. H. was put in prison for calling the Prince Regent a fat Adonis of fifty," and the idea sounds absurd enough ; but in the eyes of the law the " Examiner" article was undeniably as libellous as it was well-merited. The trial was, of course, a foregone conclusion ; and, in spite of Lord Brougham's eloquent defence, the brothers Hunt were condemned to two years' imprisonment and a fine of one thousand pounds. Leigh Hunt was confined in Horsemonger Lane Gaol from 1813 to 1815, and a great deal has been said about the bower of roses into which he turned his prison cell. Some writers have even fancied that his punishment was only nominal because he could share it with his family, his flowers, and his books. , They have ignored or forgotten that a few weeks after his release he was so much broken down that he " had not the courage to continue looking at the shoals of people passing to and fro, as the coach drove up the Strand." Just before the sentence was passed his doctor had ordered him drives in the country, and though his imprisonment brought him general sympathy and some invaluable friends, it may be doubted whether he ever recovered from the shock to his health and spirits ; while it is certain that the fine was the cause of long-continued financial embarrassments.

The visit to Italy was perhaps still more unfortunate. In 1821 the fortunes of the " Examiner " had begun to decline, and it was natural that he should be tempted by an invitation from Shelley and Lord Byron to join them in bringing out a new periodical, in which their more advanced opinions might be made public. The combination of Byron's brilliance and popularity with Hunt's experience in journalism seemed to promise fair for the venture, which was to be called "The Liberal," and it was with the brightest hopes that the Hunts set out for Italy. The terrible delays and sufferings of their voyage might well have been regarded as ominous by a superstitious spirit; but, in the first moment of reunion with Shelley, all troubles were forgotten.—And then Shelley was drowned.

The more we know of Leigh Hunt the deeper do we seem to see into this calamity, and the more clearly can we realize how it must have unstrung him for the painful necessity of working with Byron. Meanwhile that nobleman's aristocratic friends had been alarming his vanity by reflections upon his association with a *poor radical journalist.* The new journal that had seemed so attractive in prospect became distasteful in execution. Byron never admitted his change of feeling to Hunt, but he delayed the work, and, when he took it up, did it so grudgingly that failure was inevitable. Hunt, moreover, could not afford to wait, and was thus forced to receive pecuniary help from Byron, at whose invitation he had come out to live upon the proceeds of a periodical, which was now neglected by its own originator. Apart from the strain of their financial relations, the natures of Byron and Hunt were essentially incompatible, while the latter's family rather helped to widen the breach. "The

Liberal" dragged through four numbers, and then died of inanition, and its projectors separated. The Hunts remained in Italy till 1825, partly in company with Mrs. Shelley, but in the end were thankful to return to England.

In the meantime Byron died, and the public was greedy for any details of his life. The eyes of an enterprising publisher turned to Leigh Hunt, and it was agreed that he should write a biographical sketch for an edition of Byron's works. But the delight of his return to English fields led him to take too long a holiday, and in the hurry of keeping an engagement with his publisher, he had to make use of materials already in hand, so that "Lord Byron and his Contemporaries" assumed, almost by accident, the shape in which it now exists. The circumstances under which it was written coloured it with a sense of injury, not wholly wise, perhaps, but at any rate fully apologized for later by the author. It is to be observed further that Leigh Hunt's own relations with Byron had been cruelly misrepresented by earlier writers, and that his picture of "the noble poet's" character is now admitted on all hands to be true, original, and essentially kindly.

We may disregard to-day the indignation of those who would listen to nothing against Byron; and need only add that the probable cause of the continued and more reasonable complaints against the book, was the spiritual and somewhat quixotic nature of Leigh Hunt's theories concerning the rights of property, which made him regard the power to be generous as a privilege, for others as well as for himself, and led him to speak of the gifts of money he received in a manner very likely to offend the average Englishman's formal notions of financial responsibilities.[1]

During his stay in Italy, Leigh Hunt wrote a beautiful set of meditations, privately printed with the title "Christianism" (later enlarged into a book called "The Religion of the Heart"), "which represent very fully the religious side of an essentially pious nature." They are "the voice of a good heart on the lips of a beautiful speaker," whose beliefs were as tolerant as his nature was sympathetic.

He did not again leave England after his return, and later in life his affairs became less embarrassed through the generosity of the Shelley family and a royal pension, granted in 1847.

He died on August 28th, 1859. "Although his bodily powers had been giving way, his most conspicuous qualities—his memory for books, and his affection—remained ; and when his hair was white, when his ample chest had grown slender, when the very proportion of his height had visibly lessened, his step was still ready, and his dark eyes brightened at every happy expression, and at every

---

[1] A letter written to Mrs. Shelley in September, 1821, will, perhaps, illustrate most simply the way in which Leigh Hunt accepted the generosity of his friends :—" My dear Mary, Pray thank Shelley, or rather do not, for that kind part of his offer relating to the expenses. I find I have omitted it, but the instinct that led me to do so is more honourable to him than thanks. I hope you think so."
This was a gratitude that the Shelleys no doubt knew how to appreciate.

thought of kindness.  His death was simply ex-
haustion : he broke off his work to lie down and
repose.  So gentle was the final approach, that he
scarcely recognized it till the very last, and then it
came without terrors. . . . . His last breath was
used to draw from one of his sons, by minute,
eager, and searching questions all that he could
learn about the latest vicissitudes and growing
hopes of Italy,—to ask the friends and children
around him for news of those whom he loved,—
and to send love and messages to the absent who
loved him."  And so died

> "Hunt, one of those happy souls,
> Which are the salt of the earth, and without whom
> This earth would smell like what it is,—a tomb ;
> Who are what others seem."

In a critical estimate of Hunt's writings, allowance must be made for two adverse influences—the
models that his contemporaries admired, and the
pressure under which he worked.

At the time he began to write, the fatal habit of
imitating Dr. Johnson's pomposity was in vogue,
while "in poetry the Della Cruscan manner pre-
vailed, with its false simplicity and real tinsel, its
lachrymose tenderness and sham romance."  He
first imitated this artificiality, and then, by his very
detestation of it, was led to adopt a freedom of
style that sometimes degenerated into incorrectness.  If he seems to dwell upon trifles, or to
affect too much simplicity, the impulse may probably be traced to an impatience of false ideals of
dignity in writing, as the occasionally involved and

parenthetic construction of his sentences seems to arise from an intense desire for truth.

In the case of his prose work, the Herculean journalistic responsibilities that he undertook may have stood in the way of his recognition of these defects, while they must obviously have encouraged the tendency to express any idea as fully and from as many points of view as possible. When it is remembered that he had to produce copy almost daily for more than fifty years, the wonder is that so much should be worth reprinting. An explanation may be found in the great care with which he invariably wrote, in the extraordinary width of his acquaintance with the best literature, and in the fact that "he was a man of genius in a very strict sense of that word." [1]

It is a difficult matter indeed to postulate the unique beauties of his writings. They defy definition. "Versatility, clearness, lovingness, truthfulness," and absolute healthfulness are there. The touch is light and rapid, yet the deepest and widest sympathies are evinced. His pages are illuminated with passages of delicate wit and unexpected poetry, and enriched by the most happily chosen quotations.

He is most charming when writing of his friends, —Shelley, his mother, and many others that live before us in the fascinating pages of his "Autobiography." His imaginary character-sketches are scarcely less sympathetic, and, though the publication of Professor Knight's "Tales from Leigh Hunt" has perhaps shown that he was not himself

[1] Carlyle.

a master of pure fiction, it has reminded us that he can inspire fresh interest in an old story by his manner of reproducing it.   The familiar narrative assumes an added significance in his hands ; reflections, morals, side issues are suggested ; and the forgotten heroes live again before another generation, clothed in a new garb, and displaying new charms.   Nor is this all, for he can breathe life into the dry bones of an obscure chronicle, and fascinate his readers with the gossip of the past.

But the most popular of his writings have always been his purely miscellaneous essays, which depend for their subject and treatment on the suggestion of the moment :[1] as he said, in the "Wishing Cap,"—"I will take up in this paper any subject to which I feel an impulse."   And the subjects are often commonplace enough, but "he brings poetry to our breakfast-table, and strikes light out of the pebble at our feet," finding—

"Sermons in stones, and good in everything."

In these miscellaneous essays we meet with some occasional literary criticism in which "a sentence does the work of a chapter ;" thus he writes of Charles Lamb that "his essays will take their place among the daintiest productions of English wit-melancholy," and of O'Keefe that "his muse was as fresh as a dairy-maid." His longer criticisms are seldom less happy.   They are nearly always

[1] Yet those who knew him best agree in testifying that even these casual writings "were the result of very considerable labour and painstaking, of the most conscientious investigation of facts, where facts were needed ; and of a complete devotion of his faculties towards the objects to be accomplished."

*appreciations*, and yet discriminating.   He delighted to consider himself a taster in literature,
the *Indicator*, or honey-hunter, among the flowers
of the past.   He does not construct theories of
composition, but gives utterance to his delight in
an author, and makes his reader share it.   He
seems to have no prejudices,[1] though he does not
praise blindly.

His more strictly journalistic work may be estimated by a brief *résumé* of the main characteristics
of the " Examiner," which are fully set forth in its
prospectus (see vol ii.).   The independent theatrical
criticism, which he had originated in the "News,"
was here maintained, and his carefully written
miscellaneous articles gave it a literary tone, which
was unusual in newspapers of that time.   Here
also he bore witness to his admiration for the men
of real genius among his contemporaries, welcom-
ing contributions from Lamb, Hazlitt, Keats, and
Shelley, at a time when the last three were almost
entirely unknown or despised.   The same judgment was shown later in the " London Journal,"
where the writings of Bentham and Hugh Miller
received some of their earliest recognitions, and
where Carlyle's translations of Goethe were enthu-
siastically noticed.   In the " Tatler," we find him
working with Barry Cornwall, and, in the "Monthly
Repository," with W. S. Landor.

[1] This impartiality, however, cannot be claimed for the
criticism in the early numbers of the " Examiner," while he
retained two prejudices throughout life : against Dante, for
his belief in hell, and against Southey, for his complacent
Toryism.

The attitude of the " Examiner " with regard to political matters was equally advanced. " It began by being of no party, but reform gave it one ; " and although it was against the grain that Hunt ever wrote on politics, there can be no doubt that the energy and fearlessness of his editorial utterances and the consistent vigour of his paper did no little service to the cause of Liberalism in one of its darkest periods.

Turning to the consideration of his poetry, we can see the same obvious faults in it as in his prose. It is often trivial in subject, always slight in treatment, and pet ideas are sometimes allowed to run to seed. He was too much inclined to use words in unusual connections and with a meaning of his own, though without producing obscurity. It may also perhaps be criticised with less compunction than his prose, because it was his chosen work, written in times of comparative leisure, and by which he hoped to live.

But " his poetry never fails in that imaginative glow and glamour which takes us into another world than the prosaic life of every day, and enables us to forget the dullness and meanness of the actual. . . . Whatever else it may lack, it never lacks gusto,—the sense of the expression of quick, keen delight in all things naturally and wholesomely delightful." [1] His nature was essentially romantic. His thoughts kept company with brave knights and fair ladies, wandering in beautiful gardens and exchanging tender compliments. The

[1] J. A. Noble, *op. cit.*

ceremonies and customs that had grown archaic in the world of action retained their full significance in his imagination, and it was upon them that he delighted to dwell.

It is largely because he was so much at home in the fields of imagination that his poetry possesses its peculiar faults and its peculiar merits. His most perfect poems are the short Eastern tales and some of the translations, while the "Story of Rimini" well represents his genius as a whole, and is of supreme interest on account of the admiration it excited in some of the master-minds of his day.

And finally his writings are the expression of his moral nature. They are genial, sympathetic, and chivalrous like himself; revealing the main motive of his life—the desire to increase the happiness of mankind. They seem to echo the ever-memorable petition of Abou Ben Adhem :—

"Write me as one that loves his fellow-men."

REGINALD BRIMLEY JOHNSON.

CAMBRIDGE,
*February*, 1891.

# ESSAYS,

## MISCELLANEOUS, CRITICAL, AND AUTOBIOGRAPHICAL.

## DEATHS OF LITTLE CHILDREN.

["Indicator," April 5th, 1820. "Indicator and Companion," 1834. "Tale for Chimney Corner," 1869. A. Symons, 1888. C. Kent, 1889.]

A GRECIAN philosopher being asked why he wept for the death of his son, since the sorrow was in vain, replied, "I weep on that very account." And his answer became his wisdom. It is only for sophists to pretend, that we, whose eyes contain the fountains of tears, need never give way to them. It would be unwise not to do so on some occasions. Sorrow unlocks them in her balmy moods. The first bursts may be bitter and overwhelming; but the soil on which they pour, would be the worse without them. They refresh the fever of the soul —the dry misery which parches the countenance into furrows, and renders us liable to our most terrible "flesh-quakes."

I.                                                               B

There are sorrows, it is true, so great, that to give them some of the ordinary vents is to run a hazard of being overthrown. These we must rather strengthen ourselves to resist, or bow quietly and drily down, in order to let them pass over us, as the traveller does the wind of the desert. But where we feel that tears would relieve us, it is false philosophy to deny ourselves at least that first refreshment ; and it is always false consolation to tell people that because they cannot help a thing, they are not to mind it. The true way is, to let them grapple with the unavoidable sorrow, and try to win it into gentleness by a reasonable yielding. There are griefs so gentle in their very nature, that it would be worse than false heroism to refuse them a tear. Of this kind are the deaths of infants. Particular circumstances may render it more or less advisable to indulge in grief for the loss of a little child ; but, in general, parents should be no more advised to repress their first tears on such an occasion, than to repress their smiles towards a child surviving, or to indulge in any other sympathy. . It is an appeal to the same gentle tenderness ; and such appeals are never made in vain. The end of them is an acquittal from the harsher bonds of affliction—from the tying down of the spirit to one melancholy idea.

It is the nature of tears of this kind, however strongly they may gush forth, to run into quiet waters at last. We cannot easily, for the whole course of our lives, think with pain of any good and kind person whom we have lost. It is the divine nature of their qualities to conquer pain and

death itself ; to turn the memory of them into pleasure ; to survive with a placid aspect in our imaginations. We are writing at this moment just
opposite a spot which contains the grave of one in-
expressibly dear to us.[1] We see from our window
the trees about it, and the church spire. The
green fields lie around. The clouds are travelling
overhead, alternately taking away the sunshine
and restoring it. The vernal winds, piping of the
flowery summer-time, are nevertheless calling to
mind the far-distant and dangerous ocean, which
the heart that lies in that grave had many reasons
to think of. And yet the sight of this spot does
not give us pain. So far from it, it is the existence
of that grave which doubles every charm of the
spot ; which links the pleasures of our childhood
and manhood together ; which puts a hushing
tenderness in the winds, and a patient joy upon
the landscape ; which seems to unite heaven and
earth, mortality and immortality, the grass of the
tomb and the grass of the green field ; and gives a
more maternal aspect to the whole kindness of
nature. It does not hinder gaiety itself. Happiness was what its tenant, through all her troubles,
would have diffused. To diffuse happiness and to
enjoy it, is not only carrying on her wishes, but
realizing her hopes ; and gaiety, freed from its
only pollutions, malignity and want of sympathy,
is but a child playing about the knees of its
mother.

The remembered innocence and endearments of a
child stand us instead of virtues that have died older.

[1] His mother's, in Hampstead churchyard.— ED.

Children have not exercised the voluntary offices of friendship ; they have not chosen to be kind and good to us ; nor stood by us, from conscious will, in the hour of adversity. But they have shared their pleasures and pains with us as well as they could ; the interchange of good offices between us has, of necessity, been less mingled with the troubles of the world ; the sorrow arising from their death is the only one which we can associate with their memories. These are happy thoughts that cannot die. Our loss may always render them pensive ; but they will not always be painful. It is a part of the benignity of Nature that pain does not survive like pleasure, at any time, much less where the cause of it is an innocent one. The smile will remain reflected by memory, as the moon reflects the light upon us when the sun has gone into heaven.

When writers like ourselves quarrel with earthly pain (we mean writers of the same intentions, without implying, of course, anything about abilities or otherwise), they are misunderstood if they are supposed to quarrel with pains of every sort. This would be idle and effeminate. They do not pretend, indeed, that humanity might not wish, if it could, to be entirely free from pain ; for it endeavours, at all times, to turn pain into pleasure : or at least to set off the one with the other, to make the former a zest and the latter a refreshment. The most unaffected dignity of suffering does this, and, if wise, acknowledges it. The greatest benevolence towards others, the most unselfish relish of their pleasures, even at its own expense, does but

look to increasing the general stock of happiness,
though content, if it could, to have its identity
swallowed up in that splendid contemplation. We
are far from meaning that this is to be called selfish-
ness. We are far, indeed, from thinking so, or of
so confounding words. But neither is it to be
called pain when most unselfish, if disinterestedness
be truly understood. The pain that is in it softens
into pleasure, as the darker hue of the rainbow
melts into the brighter. Yet even if a harsher line
is to be drawn between the pain and pleasure of
the most unselfish mind (and ill-health,[1] for instance, may draw it), we should not quarrel with it
if it contributed to the general mass of comfort,
and were of a nature which general kindliness
could not afford. Made as we are, there are certain pains without which it would be difficult to
conceive certain great and overbalancing pleasures.
We may conceive it possible for beings to be made
entirely happy; but in our composition something
of pain seems to be a necessary ingredient, in order
that the materials may turn to as fine account as
possible, though our clay, in the course of ages and
experience, may be refined more and more. We
may get rid of the worst earth, though not of earth
itself.

Now the liability to the loss of children—or
rather what renders us sensible of it, the occasional
loss itself—seems to be one of these necessary
bitters thrown into the cup of humanity. We do

[1] For himself, he valued ill-health because "it taught me
the worth of little pleasures as well as the dignity and
utility of great pains."—"Autobiography," p. 147.—ED.

not mean that everybody must lose one of his children in order to enjoy the rest ; or that every individual loss afflicts us in the same proportion. We
allude to the deaths of infants in general. These
might be as few as we could render them. But if
none at all ever took place, we should regard every
little child as a man or woman secured ; and it will
easily be conceived what a world of endearing cares
and hopes this security would endanger. The very
idea of infancy would lose its continuity with us.
Girls and boys would be future men and women,
not present children. · They would have attained
their full growth in our imaginations, and might as
well have been men and women at once. On the
other hand, those who have lost an infant, are
never, as it were, without an infant child. They
are the only persons who, in one sense, retain it
always, and they furnish their neighbours with the
same idea.[1] The other children grow up to manhood and womanhood, and suffer all the changes
of mortality. This one alone is rendered an immortal child. Death has arrested it with his kindly
harshness, and blessed it into an eternal image of
youth and innocence.

Of such as these are the pleasantest shapes that visit
our fancy and our hopes. They are the ever-smiling
emblems of joy ; the prettiest pages that wait upon
imagination. Lastly, " Of these are the kingdom
of heaven." Wherever there is a province of that

---

[1] " I sighed," says old Captain Bolton, " when I envied
you the two bonnie children ; but I sigh not now to call
either the monk or the soldier mine own ! "—" Monastery,"
vol. iii., p. 341 ; in edition of 1830, vol. ii., p. 346.

benevolent and all-accessible empire, whether on earth or elsewhere, such are the gentle spirits that must inhabit it. To such simplicity, or the resemblance of it, must they come. Such must be the ready confidence of their hearts, and creativeness of their fancy. And so ignorant must they be of the "knowledge of good and evil," losing their discernment of that self-created trouble, by enjoying the garden before them, and not being ashamed of what is kindly and innocent.[1]

## CHILDBED.
### A PROSE POEM.

[" Monthly Repository," Nov. 1835. "Wishing Cap Papers," &c., 1874.]

AND is childbed among the graces, with its close room, and its unwilling or idle visitors, and its jesting nurse (the old and indecent stranger), and its unmotherly, and unwifely, and unlovely lamentations? Is pain so unpleasant that love cannot reconcile it? And can pleasures be repeated without shame, which are regretted with hostile cries and resentment?

No. But childbed is among the graces, with the handsome quiet of its preparation, and the smooth pillow sustaining emotion, and the soft steps of love and respect, and the room in which the breath of the universe is gratefully permitted

---

[1] One of Lamb's favourite papers. See "Autobiography," p. 250.

to enter, and mild and venerable aid, and the physician (the urbane security), and the living treasure containing treasure about to live, who looks in the eyes of him that caused it and seeks energy in the grappling of his hand, and hides her face in the pillow that she may save him a pain by stifling a greater.　There is a tear for what may have been done wrong, ever ; and what may never be to be mutually pardoned again ; but it is gone, for what needs it ?　Angelical are their whispers apart ; and Pleasure meets Pain the seraph, and knows itself to be noble in the smiling testimony of his severity.　⸎

It was on a May evening, in a cottage flowering with the greengage in the time of hyacinths and new hopes, when the hand that wrote this took the hand that had nine times laid thin and delicate on the bed of a mother's endurance ; and he kissed it, like a bride's.

L. H. 1827.

## AN EARTH UPON HEAVEN.[1]

[" The Companion," April 2nd, 1828. " Indicator and Companion," 1834. A. Symons, 1888. C. Kent, 1889.]

SOMEBODY, a little while ago, wrote an excellent article in the New Monthly Magazine on " Persons one would wish to have known." He should write another on " Persons one could wish to have dined with." There is Rabelais, and Horace, and

[1] See the poem, "A Heaven upon Earth," in vol. ii.— Ed.

the Mermaid roysters, and Charles Cotton, and Andrew Marvell, and Sir Richard Steele, *cum multis aliis :* and for the colloquial, if not the festive part, Swift and Pope, and Dr. Johnson, and Burke, and Horne Tooke. What a pity one cannot dine with them all round ! People are accused of having earthly notions of heaven. As it is difficult to have any other, we may be pardoned for thinking that we could spend a very pretty thousand years in dining and getting acquainted with all the good fellows on record ; and having got used to them, we think we could go very well on, and be content to wait some other thousands for a higher beatitude. Oh, to wear out one of the celestial lives of a triple century's duration, and exquisitely to grow old, in reciprocating dinners and teas with the immortals of old books ! Will Fielding "leave his card" in the next world ? Will Berkeley (an angel in a wig and lawn sleeves !) come to ask how Utopia gets on ? Will Shakespeare (for the greater the man, the more the good-nature might be expected) know by intuition that one of his readers (knocked up with bliss) is dying to see him at the Angel and Turk's Head, and come lounging with his hands in his doublet-pockets accordingly ?

It is a pity that none of the great geniuses, to whose lot it has fallen to describe a future state, has given us his own notions of heaven. Their accounts are all modified by the national theology ; whereas the Apostle himself has told us, that we can have no conception of the blessings intended for us. "Eye hath not seen, nor ear heard," &c.

After this, Dante's shining lights are poor. Milton's heaven, with the armed youth exercising themselves in military games, is worse. His best Paradise was on earth, and a very pretty heaven he made of it. For our parts, admitting and venerating as we do the notion of a heaven surpassing all human conception, we trust that it is no presumption to hope, that the state mentioned by the Apostle is the *final* heaven ; and that we may ascend and gradually accustom ourselves to the intensity of it, by others of a less superhuman nature. Familiar as we may be both with poetry and calamity, and accustomed to surprises and strange sights of imagination, it is difficult to fancy even the delight of suddenly emerging into a new and boundless state of existence, where everything is marvellous, and opposed to our experience. We could wish to take gently to it ; to be loosed not entirely at once. Our song desires to be " a song of degrees." Earth and its capabilities—are these nothing ? And are they to come to nothing ? Is there no beautiful realization of the fleeting type that is shown us ? No body to this shadow ? No quenching to this [drought] [1] and continued thirst ? No arrival at these natural homes and resting-places, which are so heavenly to our imaginations, even though they be built of clay, and are situate in the fields of our infancy ? We are becoming graver than we intended ; but to return to our proper style :—nothing shall persuade us, for the present, that Paradise Mount, in any pretty village in England, has not another Paradise Mount to

[1] Printed "taught" in earlier editions.—Ed.

correspond, in some less perishing region ; that is to say, provided anybody has set his heart upon it :—and that we shall not all be dining, and drinking tea, and complaining of the weather (we mean, for its not being perfectly blissful) three hundred years hence, in some snug interlunar spot, or perhaps in the moon itself, seeing that it is our next visible neighbour, and shrewdly sus- pected of being hill and dale.

It appears to us, that for a certain term of cen- turies, Heaven *must* consist of something of this kind. In a word, we cannot but persuade our- selves, that to realize everything that we have justly desired on earth, will *be* heaven ;—we mean, for that period : and that afterwards, if we behave ourselves in a proper pre-angelical manner, we shall go to another heaven, still better, where we shall realize all that we desired in our first. Of this latter we can as yet have no conception ; but of the former, we think some of the items may be as follow :—

*Imprimis,*—(not because friendship comes be- fore love in point of degree, but because it pre- cedes it, in point of time, as at school we have a male companion [1] before we are old enough to have a female)—*Imprimis* then, a friend. He will have the same tastes and inclinations as our- selves, with just enough difference to furnish argument without sharpness ; and he will be gene- rous, just, entertaining, and no shirker of his nectar. In short, he will be the best friend we

[1] As a schoolboy Leigh Hunt had very exalted notions of " Friendship." See " Juvenilia."—ED.

have had upon earth. We shall talk together " of afternoons ;" and when the *Earth* begins to rise (a great big moon, looking as happy as we know its inhabitants *will* be), other friends will join us, not so emphatically our friend as he, but excellent fellows all ; and we shall read the poets, and have some sphere-music (if we please), or renew one of our old earthly evenings, picked out of a dozen Christmases.

*Item*, a mistress. In heaven (not to speak it profanely) we know, upon the best authority, that people are "neither married nor given in marriage ;" so that there is nothing illegal in the term. (By the way, there can be no clergymen there, if there are no official duties for them. We do not say, there will be nobody who has been a clergyman. Berkeley would refute that ; and a hundred Welsh curates. But they would be no longer in orders. They would refuse to call themselves more Reverend than their neighbours.) *Item* then, a mistress ; beautiful, of course,—an angelical expression,—a Peri, or Houri, or whatever shape of perfection you choose to imagine her, and yet retaining the likeness of the woman you loved best on earth ; in fact, she herself, but completed ; all her good qualities made perfect, and all her defects taken away (with the exception of one or two charming little angelical peccadilloes, which she can only get rid of in a post-future state) ; good-tempered, laughing, serious, fond of everything about her without detriment to her special fondness for yourself, a great roamer in Elysian fields and forests, but not alone (they go in pairs there, as the jays and turtle-doves do with us); but above all things, true; oh, so true, that you take her word as you would a diamond, nothing being more transparent, or solid, or precious. Between writing some divine poem, and meeting our friends of an evening, we should walk with her, or fly (for we should have wings, of course) like a couple of human bees or doves, extracting delight from every flower, and with delight filling every shade. There is something too good in this to dwell upon; so we spare the fears and hopes of the prudish. We would lay her head upon our heart, and look more pleasure into her eyes, than the prudish or the profligate ever so much as fancied.

*Item*, books. Shakespeare and Spenser should write us *new ones!* Think of that. We would have another Decameron: and Walter Scott (for he will be there too;—we mean to beg Hume to introduce us) shall write us forty more novels, all as good as the Scotch ones; and Radical as well as Tory shall love him. It is true, we speak professionally, when we mention books.

> We think, admitted to that equal sky,
> The Arabian Nights must bear us company.

When Gainsborough died, he expired in a painter's enthusiasm, saying, "We are all going to heaven, and Vandyke is of the party."—He had a proper foretaste. Virgil had the same light, when he represented the old heroes enjoying in Elysium their favourite earthly pursuits; only one cannot help thinking, with the natural modesty of reformers, that the taste in this our interlunar heaven will be benefited from time to time by the knowledge of new-comers. We cannot well fancy a celestial ancient Briton delighting himself with painting his skin, or a Chinese angel hobbling a mile up the Milky Way in order to show herself to advantage.

For breakfast, we must have a tea beyond anything Chinese. Slaves will certainly not make the sugar; but there will be cows for the milk. One's landscapes cannot do without cows.

For horses we shall ride a Pegasus, or Ariosto's Hippogriff, or Sinbad's Roc. We mean, for our parts, to ride them all, having a passion for fabulous animals. Fable will be no fable then. We shall have just as much of it as we like; and the Utilitarians will be astonished to find how much of that sort of thing will be in request. They will look very odd, by the bye,—those gentlemen, when they first arrive; but will soon get used to the delight, and find there was more of it in their own doctrine than they imagined.

The weather will be extremely fine, but not without such varieties as shall hinder it from being tiresome. April will dress the whole country in diamonds; and there will be enough cold in winter to make a fire pleasant of an evening. The fire will be made of sweet-smelling turf and sunbeams; but it will have a look of coal. If we choose, now and then we shall even have inconveniences.

# THOUGHTS AND GUESSES ON HUMAN NATURE.

["Indicator," Sept. 13th, 1820. "Tale for Chimney Corner," 1869. A. Symons, 1888. C. Kent, 1889.]

## DEATH.

OF all impositions on the public, the greatest seems to be death. It resembles the threatening faces on each side the Treasury. Or rather, it is a necessary bar to our tendency to move forward. Nature sends us out of her hand with such an impetus towards increase of enjoyment, that something is obliged to be set up at the end of the avenue we are in, to moderate our bias, and make us enjoy the present being. Death serves to make us think, not of itself, but of what is about us.

## DEGRADING IDEAS OF DEITY.

The superstitious, in their contradictory representations of God, call him virtuous and benevolent out of the same passion of fear as induces them to make him such a tyrant. They think they shall be damned if they do not believe him the tyrant he is described:—they think they shall be damned also, if they do not gratuitously ascribe to him the virtues incompatible with damnation. Being so unworthy of praise, they think he will be particularly angry at not being praised. They shudder to think themselves better; and hasten to make amends for it, by declaring themselves as worthless as he is worthy.

## GREAT DISTINCTION TO BE MADE IN BIGOTS.

There are two sorts of religious bigots, the unhealthy and the unfeeling. The fear of the former is mixed with humanity, and they never succeed in thinking themselves favourites of God, but their sense of security is embittered, by aversions which they dare not own to themselves, and terror for the fate of those who are not so lucky. The unfeeling bigot is a mere unimaginative animal, whose thoughts are confined to the snugness of his own kennel, and who would have a good one in the next world as well as in this. He secures a place in heaven as he does in the Manchester coach or a Margate hoy. Never mind who suffers outside, woman or child. We once found ourselves by accident on board a Margate hoy, which professed to "sail by Divine Providence." Walking about the deck at night to get rid of the chillness which would occasionally visit our devotions to the starry heavens and the sparkling sea, our foot came in contact with something white, which was lying gathered up in a heap. Upon stooping down, we found it to be a woman. The methodists had secured all the beds below, and were not to be disturbed.[1]

[1] This anecdote is repeated in the "Autobiography."—ED. Leigh Hunt thinks that this whole paper was one of C. Lamb's favourites. See "Autobiography," p. 250.

# ANGLING.[1]

["Indicator," Nov. 17th, 1819. "Indicator and Companion," 1834. A. Symons, 1888. C. Kent, 1889.]

THE anglers are a race of men who puzzle us. We do not mean for their patience, which is laudable, nor for the infinite non-success of some of them, which is desirable. Neither do we agree with the good joke attributed to Swift, · that angling is always to be considered as "a stick and a string, with a fly at one end and a fool at the other." Nay, if he had books with him, and a pleasant day, we can even account for the joyousness of that prince of all punters, who, having been seen in the same identical spot one morning and evening, and asked both times whether he had had any success, said No, but in the course of the day he had had "a glorious nibble."

But the anglers boast of the innocence of their pastime ; yet it puts fellow-creatures to the torture. They pique themselves on their meditative faculties ; and yet their only excuse is a want of thought. It is this that puzzles us. Old Isaac Walton, their patriarch, speaking of his inquisitorial abstractions on the banks of a river, says,

Here we may
Think and pray,

---

[1] Leigh Hunt was constantly writing against angling. See *e. g.* "Imaginary Conversations of Pope and Swift," at the end of "Table Talk" volume.—ED.

I. C

> Before death
> Stops our breath.
> Other joys
> Are but toys,
> And to be lamented.

So saying, he "stops the breath" of a trout, by plucking him up into an element too thin to respire, with a hook and a tortured worm in his jaws—

> Other joys
> Are but toys.

If you ride, walk, or skait, or play at cricket, or at rackets, or enjoy a ball or a concert, it is "to be lamented." To put pleasure into the faces of half a dozen agreeable women, is a toy unworthy of the manliness of a worm-sticker. But to put a hook into the gills of a carp—there you attain the end of a reasonable being ; there you show your-self truly a lord of the creation. To plant your feet occasionally in the mud, is also a pleasing step. So is cutting your ankles with weeds and stones—

> Other joys
> Are but toys.

The book of Isaac Walton upon angling is undoubtedly a delightful performance in some respects. It smells of the country air, and of the flowers in cottage windows. Its pictures of rural scenery, its simplicity, its snatches of old songs, are all good and refreshing ; and his prodigious relish of a dressed fish would not be grudged him, if he had killed it a little more decently. He really seems to have a respect for a piece of sal-

mon ; to approach it, like the grace, with his hat
off.  But what are we to think of a man, who in
the midst of his tortures of other animals, is always
valuing himself on his wonderful harmlessness;
and who actually follows up one of his most complacent passages of this kind, with an injunction to
impale a certain worm twice upon the hook, because it is lively, and might get off ! All that can be
said of such an extraordinary inconsistency is, that
having been bred up in an opinion of the innocence
of his amusement, and possessing a healthy power
of exercising voluntary thoughts (as far as he had
any), he must have dozed over the opposite side of
the question, so as to become almost, perhaps
quite, insensible to it.  And angling does indeed
seem the next thing to dreaming.  It dispenses
with locomotion, reconciles contradictions, and
renders the very countenance null and void.  A
friend of ours, who is an admirer of Walton, was
struck, just as we were, with the likeness of the
old angler's face to a fish.  It is hard, angular,
and of no expression.  It seems to have been
"subdued to what it worked in ; " to have become
native to the watery element.  One might have
said to Walton, " Oh flesh, how art thou fishi-
fied ! "  He looks like a pike, dressed in broad-
cloth instead of butter.

The face of his pupil and follower, or, as he
fondly called himself, son, Charles Cotton, a poet
and a man of wit, is more good-natured and uneasy.[1]  Cotton's pleasures had not been confined

[1] The reader may see both the portraits in the late
editions of Walton.

to fishing.   His sympathies indeed had been a little superabundant, and left him, perhaps, not so great a power of thinking as he pleased.   Accordingly, we find upon the subject of angling in his writings more symptoms of scrupulousness than in those of his father.

Walton says, that an angler does no hurt but to fish ;  and this  he  counts  as  nothing.   Cotton argues, that the slaughter of them is not to be " repented ;"  and he says to his father (which looks as if the old gentleman sometimes thought upon the subject too) —

> There whilst behind some bush we wait
>   The scaly people to betray,
> We'll prove it just, with treacherous bait,
>   To make the preying trout our prey.

This argument, and another about fish's being made for " man's pleasure and diet," are all that anglers have to say for the innocence of their sport. But they are both as rank sophistications as can be ; mere beggings of the question.   To kill fish outright is a different matter.   Death is common to all ; and a trout, speedily killed by a man, may suffer no worse fate than from the jaws of a pike. It is the mode, the lingering cat-like cruelty of the angler's sport, that renders it unworthy.   If fish were made to be so treated, then men were also made to be racked and throttled by inquisitors. Indeed among other advantages of angling, Cotton reckons up a tame, fishlike acquiescence to whatever the powerful choose to inflict.

> We scratch not our pates,
> Nor repine at the rates

Our superiors impose on our living ;
But do frankly submit,
Knowing they have more wit
In demanding, than we have in giving.

Whilst quiet we sit,
We conclude all things fit,
Acquiescing with hearty submission, &c.

And this was no pastoral fiction. The anglers of those times, whose skill became famous from the celebrity of their names, chiefly in divinity, were great fallers-in with passive obedience. They seemed to think (whatever they found it necessary to say now and then upon that point) that the great had as much right to prey upon men, as the small had upon fishes ; only the men luckily had not hooks put into their jaws, and the sides of their cheeks torn to pieces. The two most famous anglers in history are Antony and Cleopatra. These extremes of the angling character are very edifying. We should like to know what these grave divines would have said to the heavenly maxim of " Do as you would be done by." Let us imagine ourselves, for instance, a sort of human fish. Air is but a rarer fluid ; and at present, in this November weather, a supernatural being who should look down upon us from a higher atmosphere, would have some reason to regard us as a kind of pedestrian carp. Now fancy a Genius fishing for us. Fancy him baiting a great hook with pickled salmon, and twitching up old Isaac Walton from the banks of the river Lee, with the hook through his ear. How he would go up, roaring and screaming, and thinking the devil had got him !

Other joys
Are but toys.

We .repeat, that if fish were made to be so treated, then we were just as much made to be racked and suffocated ; and a footpad might have argued that old Isaac was made to have his pocket picked, and be tumbled into the river. There is no end of these idle and selfish beggings of the' question, which at last argue quite as much against us as for us. And granting them, for the sake of argument, it is still obvious, on the very same ground, that men were also made to be taught better. We do not say, that all anglers are of a cruel nature ; many of them, doubtless, are amiable men in other matters. They have only never thought perhaps on that side of the question, or been accustomed from childhood to blink it. But once thinking, their amiableness and their practice become incompatible ; and if they should wish, on that account, never to have thought upon the sub-ject, they would only show, that they cared for their own exemption from suffering, and not for its diminution in general.[1]

[1] Perhaps the best thing to be said finally about angling is, that not being able to determine whether fish feel it very sensibly or otherwise, we ought to give them the benefit rather than the disadvantage of the doubt, where we *can* help it ; and our feelings the benefit, where we cannot.

# FEBRUARY.

[From the "Months," 1821, which is reprinted from the "Literary Pocket Book" of 1819.]

THE farmer now grapples with earth again, and renews the friendly contest for her treasures. He ploughs up his fallows, sows beans, pease, rye, and spring wheat, sets early potatoes, drains wet lands, dresses and repairs hedges, lops trees, and plants those kind that love a wet soil, such as poplars, alders, and willows. Here is the noblest putting in of *stock* for a nation,—the healthiest in its pursuit, and the most truly rich and returning in its *interest*.

# MARCH.

[From the "Months," 1821, which is reprinted from the "Literary Pocket Book" of 1819.]

HE sometimes, it must be confessed, as if in a fit of the spleen, hinders the buds which he has dried from blowing; and it is allowable in the less robust part of his friends out of doors, to object to the fancy he has for coming in such a cutting manner from the East. But it may be truly said, that the oftener you meet him firmly, the less he will shake you; and the more smiles you will have from the fair months that follow him.

## MAY.

[From the "Months," 1821, which is reprinted from the "Literary Pocket Book" of 1819.]

THE farmer does little but leisurely weed his garden, and enjoy the sight of his flowering industry; the sun stops long, and begins to let us feel him warmly; and when the vital sparkle of the day is over, in sight and sound, the nightingale still continues to tell us its joy; the moon seems to be watching us, as a mother does her sleeping child; and the little glowworm lights up her trusting lamp, to show her lover where she is.

## DAWN.

["Jar of Honey from Mount Hybla," 1847. Reprinted from "Ainsworth's Magazine," 1844.]

SEE also the Satyr's account of dawn [in Fletcher's "Faithful Shepherdess"], which opens with the four most exquisite lines perhaps in the whole play:

> See, the day begins to break,
> *And the light shoots like a streak*
> *Of subtle fire. The wind blows cold,*
> *While the morning doth unfold.*

Who has not felt this mingled charmingness and chilliness (we do not use the words for the sake of the alliteration) at the first opening of the morning!

Yet none but the finest poets venture upon thus combining pleasure with something that might be thought a drawback. But it is truth ; and it is truth in which the beauty surmounts the pain ; and therefore they give it. And how simple and straight-forward is every word ! There are no artificial tricks of composition here. The words are not suggested to the truth by the author, but to the author by the truth. We feel the wind blowing as simply as it does in nature ; so that if the reader be artificially trained, and does not bring a feeling for truth with him analogous to that of the poet, the very simplicity is in danger of losing him the per-ception of the beauty. And yet there is art as well as nature in the verses ; for art in the poet must perfect what nature does by her own art. Observe, for instance, the sudden and strong emphasis on the word *shoots,* and the variety of tone and modu-lation in the whole passage, and the judicious exceptions of the two *o*'s in the wind "blows cold," which have the solemn continuous sound of what it describes : also the corresponding ones in " doth unfold," which maintain the like continuity of the growing daylight. And exquisite, surely, is the dilatory and golden sound of the word " morning " between them :

> The wind blows cold,
> While the *mor*-ning doth unfold.

# FINE DAYS IN JANUARY AND FEBRUARY.[1]

["The Companion," Jan. 30th, 1828. "Indicator and Companion," 1834. C. Kent, 1889.]

E speak of those days, unexpected, sunshiny, cheerful, even vernal, which come towards the end of January, and are too apt to come alone. They are often set in the midst of a series of rainy ones, like a patch of blue in the sky. Fine weather is much at any time, after or before the end of the year ; but, in the latter case, the days are still winter days ; whereas, in the former, the year being turned, and March and April before us, we seem to feel the coming of spring. In the streets and squares, the ladies are abroad, with their colours and glowing cheeks. If you can hear anything but noise, you hear the sparrows. People anticipate at breakfast the pleasure they shall have in "getting out." The solitary poplar in a corner looks green against the sky ; and the brick wall has a warmth in it. Then in the noisier streets, what a multitude and a new life ! What horseback ! What promenading ! What shopping, and giving good day ! Bonnets encounter bonnets :—all the Miss Williamses meet all the Miss Joneses ; and everybody wonders, particularly at nothing. The shop-windows, putting forward their best, may be said to be in blossom. The yellow carriages flash in the sunshine ; foot-

[1] Cf. "Sudden fine weather," in vol. ii.

men rejoice in their white calves, not dabbed, as usual, with rain ; the gossips look out of their three-pair-of-stairs windows ; other windows are thrown open ; fruiterers' shops look well, swelling with full.baskets ; pavements are found to be dry ; lapdogs frisk under their asthmas ; and old gentle-men issue forth, peering up at the region of the north-east.

Then in the country, how emerald the green, how open-looking the prospect ! Honeysuckles (a name alone with a garden in it) are detected in blossom ; the hazel follows ; the snowdrop hangs its white perfection, exquisite with green ; we fancy the trees are already thicker ; voices of winter birds are taken for new ones ; and in Feb-ruary new ones come—the thrush, the chaffinch, and the wood-lark. Then rooks begin to pair ; and the wagtail dances in the lane. As we write this article, the sun is on our paper, and chanticleer (the same, we trust, that we heard the other day) seems to crow in a very different style, lord of the ascen-dant, and as willing to be with his wives abroad as at home. We think we see him, as in Chaucer's homestead :

> He looketh, as it were, a grim leoùn ;
> And on his toes he roameth up and down ;
> Him deigneth not to set his foot to ground ;
> He clucketh when he hath a corn yfound,
> And to him runnen then his wivès all.

Will the reader have the rest of the picture, as Chaucer gave it ? It is as bright and strong as the day itself, and as suited to it as a falcon to a knight's fist. Hear how the old poet throws forth his strenuous music; as fine, considered as mere music and versification, as the description is pleasant and noble.

> His comb was redder than the fine coràll,
> Embattled as it were a castle wall;
> His bill was black, and as the jet it shone;
> Like azure was his leggès and his tone;
> His nailès whiter than the lilly flower,
> And like the burnèd gold was his colòur.

Hardly one pause like the other throughout, and yet all flowing and sweet. The pause on the third syllable in the last line but one, and that on the sixth in the last, together with the deep variety of vowels, make a beautiful concluding couplet; and indeed the whole is a study for versification. So little were those old poets unaware of their task, as some are apt to suppose them; and so little have others dreamt, that they surpassed them in their own pretensions. The accent, it is to be observed, in those concluding words, as *coral* and *colour*, is to be thrown on the last syllable, as it is in Italian. *Colòr, colòre*, and Chaucer's old Anglo-Gallican word, is a much nobler one than our modern one *còlour*. We have injured many such words, by throwing back the accent.

We should beg pardon for this digression, if it had not been part of our understood agreement with the reader to be as desultory as we please, and as befits Companions. Our very enjoyment of the day we are describing would not let us be otherwise. It is also an old fancy of ours to associate the ideas of Chaucer with that of any early and vigorous manifestation of light and pleasure.

He is not only the "morning-star" of our poetry, as Denham called him, but the morning itself, and a good bit of the noon; and we could as soon help quoting him at the beginning of the year, as we could help wishing to hear the cry of prim-roses, and thinking of the sweet faces that buy them.

## THE WALK IN THE WOOD.

### A PROSE POEM BY A LITTLE BOY.

["Monthly Repository," Dec. 1837.]

CHILDREN are, more or less, poets by nature, they are so disposed to enjoy existence and to see the beautiful and admirable wherever they cast their eyes. And if it is not egotism in a father to think it, there is a genuine poetical feeling in the follow-ing simple and joyous observations made by a little boy, in the companiable gaiety of his heart, while strolling with him in the Bishop's Wood, between Highgate and Hampstead. He had no suspicion, of course, that he was uttering anything unusual, or that his father was taking the words down. It was a sort of human bird-song, uttered out of the fulness of comfort.]

"It would be nice to have a little house in this wood, and to walk out of it whenever we chose, and take a *little green walk.*

"You look for violets on that side, and I will look on this; *and then we shall be wanderers.*

" It is a *good joy*, having found this wood.

" Ah, you are writing :—it is convenient, that,— to be able *to write in a little green wood.*"


# A "NOW."

## DESCRIPTIVE OF A HOT DAY.

["Indicator," June 28th, 1820. "London Journal," July 23rd, 1834. "Indicator and Companion," 1834. "Tale for Chimney Corner," 1869. A. Symons, 1888. C. Kent, 1889.]

NOW the rosy-(and lazy-) fingered Aurora, issuing from her saffron house, calls up the moist vapours to surround her, and goes veiled with them as long as she can ; till Phœbus, coming forth in his power, looks everything out of the sky, and holds sharp uninterrupted empire from his throne of beams. Now the mower begins to make his sweeping cuts more slowly, and resorts oftener to the beer. Now the carter sleeps a-top of his load of hay, or plods with double slouch of shoulder, looking out with eyes winking under his shading hat, and with a hitch upward of one side of his mouth. Now the little girl at her grandmother's cottage-door watches the coaches that go by, with her hand held up over her sunny forehead. Now labourers look well resting in their white shirts at the doors of rural alehouses. Now an elm is fine there, with a seat under it ; and horses drink out of the trough, stretching their yearning necks with loosened collars ; and the traveller calls for his glass of ale, having been with-

out one for more than ten minutes; and his horse
stands wincing at the flies, giving sharp shivers of
his skin, and moving to and fro his ineffectual
docked tail; and now Miss Betty Wilson, the
host's daughter, comes streaming forth in a flowered
gown and earrings, carrying with four of her beautiful fingers the foaming glass, for which, after the
traveller has drank it, she receives with an indifferent eye, looking another way, the lawful twopence: that is to say, unless the traveller, nodding
his ruddy face, pays some gallant compliment to
her before he drinks, such as, "I'd rather kiss
you, my dear, than the tumbler," or, "I'll wait
for you, my love, if you'll marry me;" upon which,
if the man is good-looking and the lady in good-
humour, she smiles and bites her lips, and says,
"Ah, men can talk fast enough;" upon which the
old stage-coachman, who is buckling something
near her, before he sets off, says in a hoarse voice,
"So can women too for that matter," and John
Boots grins through his ragged red locks and doats
on the repartee all the day after. Now grass-
hoppers "fry," as Dryden says. Now cattle stand
in water, and ducks are envied. Now boots, and
shoes, and trees by the road-side, are thick with
dust; and dogs, rolling in it, after issuing out of the
water, into which they have been thrown to fetch
sticks, come scattering horror among the legs of
the spectators. Now a fellow who finds he has
three miles further to go in a pair of tight shoes, is
in a pretty situation. Now rooms with the sun
upon them become intolerable; and the apothe-
cary's apprentice, with a bitterness beyond aloes,

thinks of the pond he used to bathe in at school. Now men with powdered heads (especially if thick) envy those that are unpowdered, and stop to wipe them up hill, with countenances that seem to expostulate with destiny. Now boys assemble round the village pump with a ladle to it, and delight to make a forbidden splash and get wet through the shoes. Now also they make suckers of leather, and bathe all day long in rivers and ponds, and follow the fish into their cool corners and say millions of " MY eyes ! " at " tittlebats." Now the bee, as he hums along, seems to be talking heavily of the heat. Now doors and brick-walls are burning to the hand ; and a walled lane, with dust and broken bottles in it, near a brick-field, is a thing not to be thought of. Now a green lane, on the contrary, thick-set with hedge-row elms, and having the noise of a brook "rumbling in pebble-stone," is one of the pleasantest things in the world. Now youths and damsels walk through hayfields, by chance, and the latter say, " Ha' done then, William ; " and the overseer in the next field calls out to " let thic thear hay thear bide ; " and the girls persist merely to plague "such a frumpish old fellow."

Now, in town, gossips talk more than ever to one another, in rooms, in door-ways, and out of window, always beginning the conversation with saying that the heat is overpowering. Now blinds are let down, and doors thrown open, and flannel waistcoats left off, and cold meat preferred to hot, and wonder expressed why tea continues so refreshing, and people delight to sliver lettuces into bowls,

and apprentices water doorways with tin canisters
that lay several atoms of dust.   Now the water-
cart, jumbling along the middle of the street, and
jolting the showers out of its box of water, really
does something.   Now fruiterers' shops and dairies
look pleasant, and ices are the only things to those
who can get them.   Now ladies loiter in baths ;
and people make presents of flowers ; and wine is
put into ice ; and the after-dinner lounger recreates
his head with applications of perfumed water out of
long-necked bottles.   Now the lounger, who cannot resist riding his new horse, feels his boots burn
him.   Now buckskins are not the lawn of Cos. [1]
Now jockeys, walking in great-coats to lose flesh,
curse inwardly.   Now five fat people in a stage-
coach hate the sixth fat one who is coming in, and
think he has no right to be so large.   Now clerks
in office do nothing but drink soda-water and
spruce-beer, and read the newspaper.   Now the
old-clothesman drops his solitary cry more deeply
into the areas on the hot and forsaken side of the
street ; and bakers look vicious ; and cooks are
aggravated ; and the steam of a tavern-kitchen
catches hold of one like the breath of Tartarus.
Now delicate skins are beset with gnats ; and boys
make their sleeping companion start up, with
playing a burning-glass on his hand ; and blacksmiths are super-carbonated ; and cobblers in their
stalls almost feel a wish to be transplanted ; and
butter is too easy to spread ; and the dragoons
wonder whether the Romans liked their helmets ;

[1] *Coa vestis,* a thin kind of silk or gauze made in the
island of Cos, alluded to by Horace.—Ed.

I.                                                        D

and old ladies, with their lappets unpinned, walk along in a state of dilapidation ; and the servant-maids are afraid they look vulgarly hot ; and the author, who has a plate of strawberries brought him, finds that he has come to the end of his writing.

We cannot conclude this article, however, without returning thanks, both on our own account and on that of our numerous predecessors, who have left so large a debt of gratitude unpaid, to this very useful and ready monosyllable—" Now." We are sure that there is not a didactic poet, ancient or modern, who, if he possessed a decent share of candour, would not be happy to own his obligations to that masterly conjunction, which possesses the very essence of wit, for it has the art of bringing the most remote things together. And its generosity is in proportion to its wit, for it always is most profuse of its aid where it is most wanted.

We must enjoy a pleasant passage with the reader on the subject of this " eternal Now " in Beaumont and Fletcher's play of the " Woman-Hater." [1]

[1] We have not room to enjoy it here, and it is therefore omitted. The above paper was a special favourite with Keats, who contributed one or two passages to it.—" Autobiography," p. 250.—ED.

# A "NOW."

## DESCRIPTIVE OF A COLD DAY.

" Now, all amid the rigours of the year."—THOMSON.

["London Journal," Dec. 3rd, 1834. "Seer," 1840. A. Symons, 1888. C. Kent, 1889.]

A FRIEND tells us, that having written a "Now," descriptive of a hot day [see previous essay], we ought to write another, descriptive of a cold one ; and accordingly we do so. It happens that we are, at this minute, in a state at once fit and unfit for the task, being in the condition of the little boy at school, who, when asked the Latin for "cold," said he had it " at his fingers' ends ; " but this helps us to set off with a right taste of our subject ; and the fire, which is clicking in our ear, shall soon enable us to handle it comfortably in other respects.

*Now*, then, to commence.—But first, the reader who is good-natured enough to have a regard for these papers, may choose to be told of the origin of the use of this word Now, in case he is not already acquainted with it. It was suggested to us by the striking convenience it affords to descriptive writers, such as Thomson and others, who are fond of beginning their paragraphs with it, thereby saving themselves a world of trouble in bringing about a nicer conjunction of the various parts of their subject.

*Now* when the first foul torrent of the brooks—

*Now* flaming up to heaven, the potent sun—
*Now* when the cheerless empire of the sky—
But now—
When now—
Where now—
For now—&c.

We say nothing of similar words among other
nations, or of a certain *But* of the Greeks which
was as useful to them on all occasions as the *And
so* of the little children's stories.   Our business is
with our old indigenous friend.   No other *Now*
can be so present, so instantaneous, so extremely
*Now*, as our own Now.   The now of the Latins,
—*Nunc*, or *Jam*, as he sometimes calls himself,—
is a fellow of past ages.   He is no Now.   And
the *Nun* of the Greek is older.   How can there
be a *Now* which was *Then?* a " *Now-then*," as
we sometimes barbarously phrase it.   " Now *and*
then " is intelligible ; but " Now-then " is an extravagance, fit only for the delicious moments of a
gentleman about to crack his bottle, or to run
away with a lady, or to open a dance, or to carve
a turkey and chine, or to pelt snow-balls, or to
commit some other piece of ultra-vivacity, such as
excuses a man from the nicer proprieties of
language.

But to begin.  -

*Now* the moment people wake in the morning,
they perceive the coldness with their faces, though
they are warm with their bodies, and exclaim
" Here's a day ! " and pity the poor little sweep,
and the boy with the water-cresses.   How anybody can go to a cold ditch, and gather water-

cresses, seems marvellous. Perhaps we hear great
lumps in the street of something falling; and,
looking through the window, perceive the roofs of
the neighbouring houses thick with snow. The
breath is visible, issuing from the mouth as we lie.
Now we hate getting up, and hate shaving, and
hate the empty grate in one's bed-room; and
water freezes in ewers, and you may set the towel
upright on its own hardness, and the window-
panes are frost-whitened, or it is foggy, and the
sun sends a dull, brazen beam into one's room;
or, if it is fine, the windows outside are stuck with
icicles; or a detestable thaw has begun, and they
drip; but, at all events, it is horribly cold, and
delicate shavers fidget about their chambers looking distressed, and cherish their hard-hearted
enemy, the razor, in their bosoms, to warm him a
little, and coax him into a consideration of their
chins. Savage is a cut, and makes them think
destiny really too hard.

*Now* breakfast is fine; and the fire seems to
laugh at us as we enter the breakfast-room, and
say " Ha! ha! here's a better room than the bed-
chamber!" and we always poke it before we do
anything else; and people grow selfish about seats
near it; and little boys think their elders tyran-
nical for saying, " Oh, *you* don't want the fire;
your blood is young." And truly that is not the
way of stating the case, albeit young blood is
warmer than old. Now the butter is too hard to
spread; and the rolls and toast are at their maxi-
mum; and the former look glorious as they issue,
smoking, out of the flannel in which they come

from the baker's ; and people who come with
single knocks at the door are pitied ; and the
voices of boys are loud in the street, sliding or
throwing snow-balls ; and the dustman's bell
sounds cold ; and we wonder how anybody can go
about selling fish, especially with that hoarse
voice ; and schoolboys hate their slates, and blow
their fingers, and detest infinitely the no-fire at
school ; and the parish-beadle's nose is redder
than ever.

*Now* sounds in general are dull, and smoke out
of chimnies looks warm and rich, and birds are
pitied, hopping about for crumbs, and the trees
look wiry and cheerless, albeit they are still
beautiful to imaginative eyes, especially the ever-
greens, and the birch with boughs like dishevelled
hair.   Now mud in roads is stiff, and the kennel
ices over, and boys make illegal slides in the path-
ways, and ashes are strewed before doors ; or you
crunch the snow as you tread, or kick mud-flakes
before you, or are horribly muddy in cities.   But
if it is a hard frost, all the world is buttoned
up and great-coated, except ostentatious elderly
gentlemen, and pretended beggars with naked
feet ; and the delicious sound of " All hot " is
heard from roasted apple and potato stalls, the
vender himself being cold, in spite of his " hot,"
and stamping up and down to warm his feet ; and
the little boys are astonished to think how he can
eat bread and cold meat for his dinner, instead of
the smoking apples.

Now skaiters are on the alert ; the cutlers' shop-
windows abound with their swift shoes ; and as

you approach the scene of action (pond or canal) you hear the dull grinding noise of the skaits to and fro, and see tumbles, and Banbury cake-men and blackguard boys playing "hockey," and ladies standing shivering on the banks, admiring anybody but their brother, especially the gentleman who is cutting figures of eight, who, for his part, is admiring his own figure. Beginners affect to laugh at their tumbles, but are terribly angry, and long to thump the bye-standers. On thawing days, idlers persist to the last in skaiting or sliding amidst the slush and bending ice, making the Humane-Society-man ferocious. He feels as if he could give them the deaths from which it is his business to save them. When you have done skaiting, you come away feeling at once warm and numb in the feet, from the tight effect of the skaits; and you carry them with an ostentatious air of indifference, as if you had done wonders; whereas you have fairly had three slips, and can barely achieve the inside edge.

Now riders look sharp, and horses seem brittle in the legs, and old gentlemen feel so ; and coachmen, cabmen, and others, stand swinging their arms across at their sides to warm themselves ; and blacksmiths' shops look pleasant, and potato shops detestable ; the fishmongers' still more so. We wonder how he can live in that plash of wet and cold fish, without even a window. Now clerks in offices envy the one next the fire-place ; and men from behind counters hardly think themselves repaid by being called out to speak to a Countess in her chariot ; and the wheezy and effeminate pastry-cook, hatless and aproned, and with his hand in his breeches-pockets (as the graphic Cruikshank noticeth in his almanack) stands outside his door, chilling his household warmth with attending to the ice which is brought him, and seeing it un-loaded into his cellar like coals. Comfortable look the Miss Joneses, coming this way with their muffs and furs; and the baker pities the maid-servant cleaning the steps, who, for her part, says she is not cold, which he finds it difficult to believe.

Now dinner rejoiceth the gatherers together, and cold meat is despised, and the gout defieth the morrow, thinking it but reasonable on such a day to inflame itself with "t'other bottle;" and the sofa is wheeled round to the fire after dinner, and people proceed to burn their legs in their boots, and little boys their faces; and young ladies are tormented between the cold and their complexions, and their fingers freeze at the piano-forte, but they must not say so, because it will vex their poor com-fortable grand-aunt, who is sitting with her knees in the fire, and who is so anxious that they should not be spoilt.

Now the muffin-bell soundeth sweetly in the streets, reminding us, not of the man, but his muffins, and of twilight, and evening, and curtains, and the fireside. Now play-goers get cold feet, and invalids stop up every crevice in their rooms, and make themselves worse; and the streets are comparatively silent; and the wind rises and falls in moanings; and fires burn blue and crackle; and an easy-chair with your feet by it on a stool, the lamp or candles a little behind you, and an interesting book just opened where you left off, is a bit of heaven upon earth. People in cottages crowd close into the chimney, and tell stories of ghosts and murders, the blue flame affording something like evidence of the facts.

" The owl, with all her feathers, is a-cold," [1]

or you think her so. The whole country feels like a petrifaction of slate and stillness, cut across by the wind ; and nobody in the mail-coach is warm but the horses, who steam pitifully when they stop. The " oldest man " makes a point of never having "seen such weather." People have a painful doubt whether they have any chins or not ; ears ache with the wind ; and the waggoner, setting his teeth together, goes puckering up his cheeks, and thinking the time will never arrive when he shall get to the Five Bells.

At night, people get sleepy with the fireside, and long to go to bed, yet fear it on account of the different temperature of the bed-room ; which is furthermore apt to wake them up. Warming-pans and hot-water bottles are in request ; and naughty boys eschew their night-shirts, and go to bed in their socks.

" Yes," quoth a little boy, to whom we read this passage, " and make their younger brother go to bed first."

[1] Keats, in the " Eve of St. Agnes." Mr. Keats gave us some touches in our account of the " Hot Day " (first published in the " Indicator ") as we sat writing it in his company, alas ! how many years back. We have here made him contribute to our " Cold Day." Thus it is to have immortal friends whose company never forsakes us.

# GETTING UP ON COLD MORNINGS.[1]

["Indicator," Jan. 19th, 1820.  "Indicator and Companion," 1834.  "Tale for a Chimney Corner," 1869.  A. Symons, 1888.]

AN Italian author—Giulio Cordara, a Jesuit—has written a poem upon insects, which he begins by insisting, that those troublesome and abominable little animals were created for our annoyance, and that they were certainly not inhabitants of Paradise. We of the north may dispute this piece of theology; but on the other hand, it is as clear as the snow on the house-tops, that Adam was not under the necessity of shaving; and that when Eve walked out of her delicious bower, she did not step upon ice three inches thick.

Some people say it is a very easy thing to get up of a cold morning. You have only, they tell you, to take the resolution; and the thing is done. This may be very true; just as a boy at school has only to take a flogging, and the thing is over. But we have not at all made up our minds upon it ; and we find it a very pleasant exercise to discuss the matter, candidly, before we get up. This at least is not idling, though it may be lying. It affords an excellent answer to those, who ask how lying in bed can be indulged in by a reasoning being,—a rational creature. How ? Why with

---

[1] The other side of the argument is given in the "Seer," No. VIII., under the title, "A word on early rising."—ED.

the argument calmly at work in one's head, and the clothes over one's shoulder. Oh—it is a fine way of spending a sensible, impartial half-hour.

If these people would be more charitable, they would get on with their argument better. But they are apt to reason so ill, and to assert so dogmatically, that one could wish to have them stand round one's bed of a bitter morning, and lie before their faces. They ought to hear both sides of the bed, the inside and out. If they cannot entertain themselves with their own thoughts for half an hour or so, it is not the fault of those who can. If their will is never pulled aside by the enticing arms of imagination, so much the luckier for the stage-coachman.

Candid inquiries into one's decumbency, besides the greater or less privileges to be allowed a man in proportion to his ability of keeping early hours, the work given his faculties, &c., will at least concede their due merits to such representations as the following. In the first place, says the injured but calm appealer, I have been warm all night, and find my system in a state perfectly suitable to a warm-blooded animal. To get out of this state into the cold, besides the inharmonious and uncritical abruptness of the transition, is so unnatural to such a creature, that the poets, refining upon the tortures of the damned, make one of their greatest agonies consist in being suddenly transported from heat to cold,—from fire to ice. They are "haled" out of their "beds," says Milton, by "harpy-footed furies,"—fellows who come to call them. On my first movement towards the anticipation of getting up, I find that such parts of the sheets and bolster, as are exposed to the air of the room, are stone-cold. On opening my eyes, the first thing that meets them is my own breath rolling forth, as if in the open air, like smoke out of a cottage chimney. Think of this symptom. Then I turn my eyes sideways and see the window all frozen over. Think of that. Then the servant comes in. "It is very cold this morning, is it not?"—"Very cold, Sir."—"Very cold indeed, isn't it?"— "Very cold indeed, Sir."—"More than usually so, isn't it, even for this weather?" (Here the servant's wit and good-nature are put to a considerable test, and the inquirer lies on thorns for the answer.) "Why, Sir . . . . I think it *is*." (Good creature! There is not a better, or more truth-telling servant going.) "I must rise, however—get me some warm water."—Here comes a fine interval between the departure of the servant and the arrival of the hot water; during which, of course, it is of "no use" to get up. The hot water comes. "Is it quite hot?"—"Yes, Sir."—"Perhaps too hot for shaving: I must wait a little?"— "No, Sir; it will just do." (There is an over-nice propriety sometimes, an officious zeal of virtue, a little troublesome.) "Oh—the shirt— you must air my clean shirt;—linen gets very damp this weather."—"Yes, Sir." Here another delicious five minutes. A knock at the door. "Oh, the shirt—very well. My stockings—I think the stockings had better be aired too."— "Very well, Sir."—Here another interval. At length everything is ready, except myself. I now,

continues our incumbent (a happy word, by the
bye, for a country vicar)—I now cannot help
thinking a good deal—who can?—upon the unnecessary and villainous custom of shaving : it is a
thing so unmanly (here I nestle closer)—so effeminate (here I recoil from an unlucky step into the
colder part of the bed.)—No wonder that the
Queen of France took part with the rebels against
that degenerate King, her husband, who first
affronted her smooth visage with a face like her
own.) The Emperor Julian never showed the
luxuriancy of his genius to better advantage than in
reviving the flowing beard. Look at Cardinal
Bembo's picture—at Michael Angelo's—at Titian's
—at Shakespeare's—at Fletcher's—at Spenser's—
at Chaucer's—at Alfred's—at Plato's—I could
name a great man for every tick of my watch.—
Look at the Turks, a grave and otiose people.—
Think of Haroun Al Raschid and Bed-ridden
Hassan.—Think of Wortley Montague, the worthy
son of his mother, a man above the prejudice of
his time.—Look at the Persian gentlemen, whom
one is ashamed of meeting about the suburbs, their
dress and appearance are so much finer than our
own.—Lastly, think of the razor itself—how
totally opposed to every sensation of bed—how
cold, how edgy, how hard ! how utterly different
from anything like the warm and circling ampli-
tude, which

> Sweetly recommends itself
> Unto our gentle senses.

Add to this, benumbed fingers, which may help
you to cut yourself, a quivering body, a frozen

towel, and a ewer full of ice; and he that says there is nothing to oppose in all this, only shows, at any rate, that he has no merit in opposing it.

Thomson the poet, who exclaims in his Seasons—

Falsely luxurious! Will not man awake?

used to lie in bed till noon, because he said he had no motive in getting up. He could imagine the good of rising; but then he could also imagine the good of lying still; and his exclamation, it must be allowed, was made upon summer-time, not winter. We must proportion the argument to the individual character. A money-getter may be drawn out of his bed by three and four pence; but this will not suffice for a student. A proud man may say, "What shall I think of myself, if I don't get up?" but the more humble one will be content to waive this prodigious notion of himself, out of respect to his kindly bed. The mechanical man shall get up without any ado at all; and so shall the barometer. An ingenious lier in bed will find hard matter of discussion even on the score of health and longevity. He will ask us for our proofs and precedents of the ill effects of lying later in cold weather; and sophisticate much on the advantages of an even temperature of body; of the natural propensity (pretty universal) to have one's way; and of the animals that roll themselves up, and sleep all the winter. As to longevity, he will ask whether the longest life is of necessity the best; and whether Holborn is the handsomest street in London.

We only know of one confounding, not to say confounded argument, fit to overturn the huge luxury, the "enormous bliss"—of the vice in question. A lier in bed may be allowed to profess a disinterested indifference for his health or longevity ; but while he is showing the reasonableness of consulting his own or one person's comfort, he must admit the proportionate claim of more than one ; and the best way to deal with him is this, especially for a lady ; for we earnestly recommend the use of that sex on such occasions, if not somewhat *over*-persuasive ; since extremes have an awkward knack of meeting. First then, admit all the ingeniousness of what he says, telling him that the bar has been deprived of an excellent lawyer. Then look at him in the most good-natured manner in the world, with a mixture of assent and appeal in your countenance, and tell him that you are waiting breakfast for him ; that you never like to breakfast without him ; that you really want it too ; that the servants want theirs ; that you shall not know how to get the house into order, unless he rises ; and that you are sure he would do things twenty times worse, even·than getting out of his warm bed, to put them all into good humour and a state of comfort. Then, after having said·this, throw in the comparatively indifferent matter, to *him*, about his health ; but tell him that it is no indifferent matter to you ; that the sight of his illness makes more people suffer than one ; but that if, nevertheless, he really does feel so very sleepy and so very much refreshed by—— Yet stay ; we hardly know whether the frailty of a—— Yes, yes ; say that too, especially if you say it with sincerity ; for if the weakness of human nature on the one hand and the *vis inertiæ* on the other, should lead him to take advantage of it once or twice, good-humour and sincerity form an irresistible junction at last ; and are still better and warmer things than pillows and blankets.

Other little helps of appeal may be thrown in, as occasion requires. You may tell a lover, for instance, that lying in bed makes people corpulent ; a father, that you wish him to complete the fine manly example he sets his children ; a lady, that she will injure her bloom or her shape, which M. or W. admires so much ; and a student or artist, that he is always so glad to have done a good day's work, in his best manner.

*Reader.* And pray, Mr. Indicator, how do *you* behave yourself in this respect ?

*Indic.* Oh, Madam, perfectly, of course ; like all advisers.

*Reader.* Nay, I allow that your mode of argument does not look quite so suspicious as the old way of sermonizing and severity, but I have my doubts, especially from that laugh of yours. If I should look in to-morrow morning—

*Indic.* Ah, Madam, the look in of a face like yours does anything with me. It shall fetch me up at nine, if you please—*six*, I meant to say.

## - THE OLD GENTLEMAN..

[" Indicator," Feb. 2nd, 1820. "Tale for a Chimney Corner," 1869. A. Symons, 1888. C. Kent, 1889.]

UR Old Gentleman, in order to be exclusively himself, must be either a widower or a bachelor. Suppose the former. We do not mention his precise age, which would be invidious :—nor whether he wears his own hair or a wig; which would be wanting in universality. If a wig, it is a compromise between the more modern scratch and the departed glory of the toupee. If his own hair, it is white, in spite of his favourite grandson, who used to get on the chair behind him, and pull the silver hairs out, ten years ago. If he is bald at top, the hairdresser, hovering and breathing about him like a second youth, takes care to give the bald place as much powder as the covered; in order that he may convey to the 'sensorium within a pleasing indistinctness of idea respecting the exact limits of skin and hair. He is very clean and neat; and, in warm weather, is proud of opening his waistcoat half-way down, and letting so much of his frill be seen, in order to show his hardiness as well as taste. His watch and shirt-buttons are of the best; and he does not care if he has two rings on a finger. If his watch ever failed him at the club or coffee-house, he would take a walk every day to the nearest clock of good character, purely to keep it right. He has a cane at home, but seldom uses it, on finding it out of fashion with his elderly juniors. He has a small cocked hat for gala days, which he lifts higher from his head than the round one, when made a bow to. In his pockets are two handkerchiefs (one for the neck at night-time), his spectacles, and his pocket-book. The pocket-book, among other things, contains a receipt for a cough, and some verses cut out of an odd sheet of an old magazine, on the lovely Duchess of A., beginning—

**When beauteous Mira walks the plain.**

He intends this for a common-place book which he keeps, consisting of passages in verse and prose, cut out of newspapers and magazines, and pasted in columns; some of them rather gay. His principal other books [1] are Shakespeare's Plays and Milton's Paradise Lost; the Spectator, the History of England, the Works of Lady M. W. Montague, Pope and Churchill; Middleton's Geography; the Gentleman's Magazine; Sir John Sinclair on Longevity; several plays with portraits in character; Account of Elizabeth Canning, Memoirs of George Ann Bellamy, Poetical Amusements at Bath-Easton, Blair's Works, Elegant Extracts; Junius as originally published; a few pamphlets on the American War and Lord George Gordon, &c., and one on the French Revolution. In his sitting-rooms are some engravings from Hogarth and Sir Joshua; an engraved por-

[1] This is only one of the numerous· proofs—in his books and letters—of the width of Leigh Hunt's own acquaintance with literature, which would suggest to him at once books suitable for any taste or subject.—ED.

trait of the Marquis of Granby; ditto of M. le Comte de Grasse surrendering to Admiral Rodney; a humorous piece after Penny; and a portrait of himself, painted by Sir Joshua. His wife's portrait is in his chamber, looking upon his bed. She is a little girl, stepping forward with a smile, and a pointed toe, as if going to dance. He lost her when she was sixty.

The Old Gentleman is an early riser, because he intends to live at least twenty years longer. He continues to take tea for breakfast, in spite of what is said against its nervous effects; having been satisfied on that point some years ago by Dr. Johnson's criticism on Hanway, and a great liking for tea previously. His china cups and saucers have been broken since his wife's death, all but one, which is religiously kept for his use. He passes his morning in walking or riding, looking in at auctions, looking after his India bonds or some such money securities, furthering some subscription set on foot by his excellent friend Sir John, or cheapening a new old print for his portfolio. He also hears of the newspapers; not caring to see them till after dinner at the coffee-house. He may also cheapen a fish or so; the fishmonger soliciting his doubting eye as he passes, with a profound bow of recognition. He eats a pear before dinner.

His dinner at the coffee-house is served up to him at the accustomed hour, in the old accustomed way, and by the accustomed waiter. If William did not bring it, the fish would be sure to be stale, and the flesh new. He eats no tart; or if he ventures on a little, takes cheese with it. You might as soon attempt to persuade him out of his senses, as that cheese is not good for digestion. He takes port; and if he has drunk more than usual, and in a more private place, may be induced by some respectful inquiries respecting the old style of music, to sing a song composed by Mr. Oswald or Mr. Lampe, such as—

or
> **Chloe, by that borrowed kiss,**
>
> **Come, gentle god of soft repose,**

or his wife's favourite ballad, beginning—

> **At Upton on the hill,**
> **There lived a happy pair.**

Of course, no such exploit can take place in the coffee-room: but he will canvass the theory of that matter there with you, or discuss the weather, or the markets, or the theatres, or the merits of "my lord North" or "my lord Rockingham;" for he rarely says simply, lord; it is generally "my lord," trippingly and genteelly off the tongue. If alone after dinner, his great delight is the newspaper; which he prepares to read by wiping his spectacles, carefully adjusting them on his eyes, and drawing the candle close to him, so as to stand sideways betwixt his ocular aim and the small type. He then holds the paper at arm's length, and dropping his eyelids half down and his mouth half open, takes cognizance of the day's information. If he leaves off, it is only when the door is opened by a new-comer, or when he suspects somebody is over-anxious to get the paper out of

his hand. On these occasions he gives an important hem ! or so ; and resumes.

In the evening, our Old Gentleman is fond
of going to the theatre, or of having a game of
cards. If he enjoys the latter at his own house or
lodgings, he likes to play with some friends whom
he has known for many years ; but an elderly
stranger may be introduced, if quiet and scientific;
and the privilege is extended to younger men of
letters ; who, if ill players, are good losers. Not
that he is a miser, but to win money at cards is
like proving his victory by getting the baggage ;
and to win of a younger man is a substitute for his
not being able to beat him at rackets. He breaks
up early, whether at home or abroad.

At the theatre, he likes a front row in the pit.
He comes early, if he can do so without getting
into a squeeze, and sits patiently waiting for the
drawing up of the curtain, with his hands placidly
lying one over the other on the top of his stick.
He generously admires some of the best performers, but thinks them far inferior to Garrick,
Woodward, and Clive. During splendid scenes,
he is anxious that the little boy should see.

He has been induced to look in at Vauxhall
again, but likes it still less than he did years back,
and cannot bear it in comparison with Ranelagh.
He thinks everything looks poor, flaring, and
jaded. "Ah !" says he, with a sort of triumphant
sigh, "Ranelagh was a noble place ! Such taste,
such elegance, such beauty ! There was the Duchess
of A., the finest woman in England, Sir ; and Mrs.
L., a mighty fine creature ; and Lady Susan what's

her name, that had that unfortunate affair with Sir
Charles. Sir, they came swimming by you like the
swans."

The Old Gentleman is very particular in having
his slippers ready for him at the fire, when he
comes home. He is also extremely choice in his
snuff, and delights to get a fresh boxfull in
Tavistock-street, in his way to the theatre. His
box is a curiosity from India. He calls favourite
young ladies by their Christian names, however
slightly acquainted with them; and has a privilege
also of saluting all brides, mothers, and indeed
every species of lady, on the least holiday occasion.
If the husband for instance has met with a piece
of luck, he instantly moves forward, and gravely
kisses the wife on the cheek. The wife then says,
" My niece, Sir, from the country;" and he kisses
the niece. The niece, seeing her cousin biting her
lips at the joke, says, " My cousin Harriet, Sir ; "
and he kisses the cousin. He " never recollects
such weather," except during the " Great Frost,"
or when he rode down with "Jack Skrimshire to
Newmarket." He grows young again in his little
grandchildren, especially the one which he thinks
most like himself; which is the handsomest. Yet
he likes best perhaps the one most resembling his
wife ; and will sit with him on his lap, holding his
hand in silence, for a quarter of an hour together.
He plays most tricks with the former, and makes
him sneeze. He asks little boys in general who
was the father of Zebedee's children. If his grand-
sons are at school, he often goes to see them; and
makes them blush by telling the master or the

upper-scholars, that they are fine boys, and of a precocious genius. He is much struck when an old acquaintance dies, but adds that he lived too fast; and that poor Bob was a sad dog in his youth; "a very sad dog, Sir; mightily set upon a short life and a merry one."

When he gets very old indeed, he will sit for whole evenings, and say little or nothing; but informs you, that there is Mrs. Jones (the housekeeper)—"*She*'ll talk."

## THE OLD LADY.

["The Round Table," No. 45, in the "Examiner," Sept. 29th, 1816. "Indicator," Nov. 29th, 1820. "Indicator and Companion," 1834. A. Symons, 1888. C. Kent, 1889.]

IF the Old Lady is a widow and lives alone, the manners of her condition and time of life are so much the more apparent. She generally dresses in plain silks, that make a gentle rustling as she moves about the silence of her room; and she wears a nice cap with a lace border, that comes under the chin. In a placket at her side is an old enamelled watch, unless it is locked up in a drawer of her toilet, for fear of accidents. Her waist is rather tight and trim than otherwise, as she had a fine one when young; and she is not sorry if you see a pair of her stockings on a table, that you may be aware of the neatness of her leg and foot. Contented with these and other evident indications of a good shape, and letting her young friends understand that she can afford to obscure it a little, she wears pockets, and uses them well too. In the one is her handkerchief, and any heavier matter that is not likely to come out with it, such as the change of a sixpence ; in the other is a miscellaneous assortment, consisting of a pocket-book, a bunch of keys, a needle-case, a spectacle-case, crumbs of biscuit, a nutmeg and grater, a smelling-bottle, and, according to the season, an orange or apple, which after many days she draws out, warm and glossy, to give to some little child that has well behaved itself. She generally occupies two rooms, in the neatest condition possible. In the chamber is a bed with a white coverlet, built up high and round, to look well, and with curtains of a pastoral pattern, consisting alternately of large plants, and shepherds and shepherdesses. On the mantelpiece are more shepherds and shepherdesses, with dot-eyed sheep at their feet, all in coloured ware : the man, perhaps, in a pink jacket and knots of ribbons at his knees and shoes, holding his crook lightly in one hand, and with the other at his breast, turning his toes out and looking tenderly at the shepherdess : the woman holding a crook also, and modestly returning his look, with a gipsy-hat jerked up behind, a very slender waist, with petticoat and hips to *counteract,* and the petticoat pulled up through the pocket-holes, in order to show the trimness of her ankles. But these patterns, of course, are various. The toilet is ancient, carved at the edges, and tied about with a snow-white drapery of muslin. Beside it are various boxes, mostly japan ; and the set of drawers are exquisite things for a little girl to rummage, if ever little girl be so bold,—containing ribbons and laces of various kinds ; linen smelling of lavender, of the flowers of which there is always dust in the corners ; a heap of pocket-books for a series of years ; and pieces of dress long gone by, such as head-fronts, stomachers, and flowered satin shoes, with enormous heels. The stock of *letters* are under especial lock and key. So much for the bed-room. In the sitting-room is rather a spare assortment of shining old mahogany furniture, or carved arm-chairs equally old, with chintz draperies down to the ground ; a folding or other screen, with Chinese figures, their round, little-eyed, meek faces perking sideways ; a stuffed bird, perhaps in a glass case (a living one is too much for her) ; a portrait of her husband over the mantelpiece, in a coat with frog-buttons, and a delicate frilled hand lightly inserted in the waistcoat ; and opposite him on the wall, is a piece of embroidered literature, framed and glazed, containing some moral distich or maxim, worked in angular capital letters, with two trees or parrots below, in their proper colours ; the whole concluding with an A B C and numerals, and the name of the fair industrious, expressing it to be " her work, Jan. 14, 1762." The rest of the furniture consists of a looking-glass with carved edges, perhaps a settee, a hassock for the feet, a mat for the little dog, and a small set of shelves, in which are the " Spectator " and " Guardian," the " Turkish Spy," a Bible and Prayer Book, Young's " Night Thoughts " with a piece of lace in it to flatten, Mrs. Rowe's " Devout Exercises of the Heart," Mrs. Glasse's " Cookery," and perhaps "Sir Charles Grandison," and "Clarissa." "John Buncle" is in the closet among the pickles and preserves. The clock is on the landing-place between the two room doors, where it ticks audibly but quietly ; and the landing-place, as well as the stairs, is carpeted to a nicety. The house is most in character, and properly coeval, if it is in a retired suburb, and strongly built, with wainscot rather than paper inside, and lockers in the windows. Before the windows should be some quivering poplars. Here the Old Lady receives a few quiet visitors to tea, and perhaps an early game at cards : or you may see her going out on the same kind of visit herself, with a light umbrella running up into a stick and crooked ivory handle, and her little dog, equally famous for his love to her and captious antipathy to strangers. Her grandchildren dislike him on holidays, and the boldest sometimes ventures to give him a sly kick under the table. When she returns at night, she appears, if the weather happens to be doubtful, in a calash ; and her servant in pattens, follows half behind and half at her side, with a lantern.

Her opinions are not many nor new. She thinks the clergyman a nice man. The Duke of Wellington, in her opinion, is a very great man ; but she has a secret preference for the Marquis of Granby. She thinks the young women of the present day too forward, and the men not respectful enough ; but hopes her grandchildren will be better ; though she differs with her daughter in several points respecting their management. She sets little value on the new accomplishments ; is a great though delicate connoisseur in butcher's meat and all sorts of housewifery ; and if you mention waltzes, expatiates on the grace and fine breeding of the minuet. She longs to have seen one danced by Sir Charles Grandison, whom she almost considers as a real person. She likes a walk of a summer's evening, but avoids the new streets, canals, &c., and sometimes goes through the churchyard, where her other children and her husband lie buried, serious, but not melancholy. She has had three great epochs in her life :—her marriage—her having been at court, to see the King and Queen and Royal Family—and a compliment on her figure she once received, in passing, from Mr. Wilkes, whom she describes as a sad, loose man, but engaging. His plainness she thinks much exaggerated. If anything takes her at a distance from home, it is still the court ; but she seldom stirs, even for that. The last time but one that she went, was to see the Duke of Wirtemberg ; and most probably for the last time of all, to see the Princess Charlotte and Prince Leopold. From this beatific vision she returned with the same admiration as ever for the fine comely appearance of the Duke of York and the rest of the family, and great delight at having had a near view of the Princess, whom she speaks of with smiling pomp and lifted mittens, clasping them as passionately as she can together, and calling her, in a transport of mixed loyalty and self-love, a fine royal young creature, and " Daughter of England."[1]

[1] This and "The Old Gentleman" were favourite papers of Lord Holland's. See "Autobiography," p. 250.

# THE MAID-SERVANT.[1]

[. ["The Round Table," No. 46, in the "Examiner," Oct.
20th, 1816.  "Indicator," Nov. 22nd, 1820.  "Indicator
and Companion," 1834.]

**M**UST be considered as young, or else she
has married the butcher, the butler, or
*her cousin*, or has otherwise settled into
a character distinct from her original
one, so as to become what is properly called the
domestic.   The Maid-servant, in her apparel, is
either slovenly and fine by turns, and dirty always ;
or she is at all times snug and neat, and dressed
according to her station.   In the latter case, her
ordinary dress is black stockings, a stuff gown, a
cap, and a neck-handkerchief pinned cornerwise
behind.   If you want a pin, she just feels about
her, and has always one to give you.   On Sundays
and holidays, and perhaps of afternoons, she
changes her black stockings for white, puts on a
gown of a better texture and fine pattern, sets her
cap and her curls jauntily, and lays aside the neck-
handkerchief for a high-body, which, by the way,
is not half so pretty.   There is something very
warm and latent in the handkerchief—something
easy, vital, and genial. A woman in a high-bodied
gown, made to fit her like a case, is by no means
more modest, and is much less tempting.  She looks

In some respects, particularly of costume, this portrait
must be understood of originals existing twenty or thirty
years ago.

like a figure at the head of a ship. We could almost see her chucked out of doors into a cart, with
as little remorse as a couple of sugar-loaves. The
tucker is much better, as well as the handkerchief,
and is to the other what the young lady is to the
servant. The one always reminds us of the Sparkler
in Sir Richard Steele; the other .of Fanny in
" Joseph Andrews."

But to return. The general furniture of her ordinary room, the kitchen, is not so much her own as
her Master's and Mistress's, and need not be described : but in a drawer of the dresser or the table, in
company with a duster and a pair of snuffers, may be
found some of her property, such as a brass thimble,
a pair of scissors, a thread-case, a piece of wax
much wrinkled with the thread, an odd volume of
" Pamela," and perhaps a sixpenny play, such as
"George Barnwell," or Mrs. Behn's "Oroonoko."
There is a piece of looking-glass in the window.
The· rest of her furniture is in the garret, where
you may find a good looking-glass on the table ;
and in the window a Bible, a comb, and a piece of
soap. Here stands also, under stout lock and key,
the mighty mystery,—the box,—containing, among
other things, her clothes, two or three song-books,
consisting of nineteen for the penny ; sundry Tragedies at a halfpenny the sheet ; the " Whole Nature
of Dreams Laid Open," together with the " For-
tune-teller " and the " Account of the Ghost of
Mrs. Veal ; " the " Story of the Beautiful Zoa "
" who was cast away on a desart island, showing
how," &c. ; some half-crowns in a purse, including
pieces of country-money, with the good Countess of

Coventry on one of them, riding naked on the horse; a silver penny wrapped up in cotton by itself; a crooked sixpence, given her before she came to town, and the giver of which has either forgotten or been forgotten by her, she is not sure which;—two little enamel boxes, with looking-glass in the lids, one of them a fairing, the other "a Trifle from Margate;" and lastly, various letters, square and ragged, and directed in all sorts of spellings, chiefly with little letters for capitals. One of them, written by a girl who went to a day-school, is directed " Miss."

In her manners, the Maid-servant sometimes imitates her young mistress; she puts her hair in papers, cultivates a shape, and occasionally contrives to be out of spirits. But her own character and condition overcome all sophistications of this sort; her shape, fortified by the mop and scrubbing-brush, will make its way; and exercise keeps her healthy and cheerful. From the same cause her temper is good; though she gets into little heats when a stranger is over-saucy, or when she is told not to go so heavily down stairs, or when some unthinking person goes up her wet stairs with dirty shoes,—or when she is called away often from dinner; neither does she much like to be seen scrubbing the street-door steps of a morning; and sometimes she catches herself saying, " Drat that butcher," but immediately adds, " God forgive me." The tradesmen indeed, with their compliments and arch looks, seldom give her cause to complain. The milkman bespeaks her good-humour for the day with " Come, pretty maids: "

—then follow the butcher, the baker, the oilman, &c., all with their several smirks and little loiterings; and when she goes to the shops herself, it is for her the grocer pulls down his string from its roller with more than the ordinary whirl, and tosses his parcel into a tie.

Thus pass the mornings between working, and singing, and giggling, and grumbling, and being flattered. If she takes any pleasure unconnected with her office before the afternoon, it is when she runs up the area-steps or to the door to hear and purchase a new song, or to see a troop of soldiers go by; or when she happens to thrust her head out of a chamber window at the same time with a servant at the next house, when a dialogue infallibly ensues, stimulated by the imaginary obstacles between. If the Maid-servant is wise, the best part of her work is done by dinner-time; and nothing else is necessary to give perfect zest to the meal. She tells us what she thinks of it, when she calls it "a bit o' dinner." There is the same sort of eloquence in her other phrase, "a cup o' tea;" but the old ones, and the washerwomen, beat her at that. After tea in great houses, she goes with the other servants to hot cockles, or What-are-my-thoughts-like, and tells Mr. John to "have done then;" or if there is a ball given that night, they throw open the doors, and make use of the music up stairs to dance by. In smaller houses, she receives the visits of her aforesaid cousin; and sits down alone, or with a fellow maid-servant, to work; talks of her young master or mistress and Mr. Ivins (Evans); or else she calls to mind her own friends in the country ; where she thinks the cows and " all that " beautiful, now she is away. Meanwhile, if she is lazy, she snuffs the candle with her scissors ; or if she has eaten more heartily than usual, she sighs double the usual number of times, and thinks that tender hearts were born to be unhappy.

Such being the Maid-servant's life in-doors, she scorns, when abroad, to be anything but a creature of sheer enjoyment. The Maid-servant, the sailor, and the school-boy, are the three beings that enjoy a holiday beyond all the rest of the world ;—and all for the same reason,—because their inexperience, peculiarity of life, and habit of being with persons of circumstances or thoughts above them, give them all, in their way, a cast of the romantic. The most active of the money-getters is a vegetable compared with them. The Maid-servant when she first goes to Vauxhall, thinks she is in heaven. A theatre is all pleasure to her, whatever is going forward, whether the play or the music, or the waiting which makes others impatient, or the munching of apples and gingerbread, which she and her party commence almost as soon as they have seated themselves. She prefers tragedy to comedy, because it is grander, and less like what she meets with in general ; and because she thinks it more in earnest also, especially in the love-scenes. Her favourite play is "Alexander the Great, or the Rival Queens." Another great delight is in going a shopping. She loves to look at the pictures in the windows, and the fine things labelled with those corpulent numerals of " only 7s."—" only 6s. 6d."

She has also, unless born and bred in London, been to see my Lord Mayor, the fine people coming out of Court, and the "beasties" in the Tower; and at all events she has been to Astley's and the Circus, from which she comes away, equally smitten with the rider, and sore with laughing at the clown. But it is difficult to say what pleasure she enjoys most. One of the completest of all is the fair, where she walks through an endless round of noise, and toys, and gallant apprentices, and wonders. Here she is invited in by courteous and well-dressed people, as if she were a mistress. Here also is the conjuror's booth, where the operator himself, a most stately and genteel person all in white, calls her Ma'am; and says to John by her side, in spite of his laced hat, "Be good enough, sir, to hand the card to the lady."

Ah! may her "cousin" turn out as true as he says he is; or may she get home soon enough and smiling enough to be as happy again next time.

# THE WAITER

[" London Journal," June 13th, 1835. " Seer," 1840. A. Symons, 1888. C. Kent, 1889.]

GOING into the City the other day upon business, we took a chop at a tavern, and renewed our acquaintance, after years of interruption, with that swift and untiring personage, yclept a waiter. We mention this long interval of acquaintance, in order to

account for any deficiencies that may be found in
our description of him. Our readers perhaps will
favour us with a better. He is a character before
the public : thousands are acquainted with him,
and can fill up the outline. But we felt irresistibly
impelled to sketch him ; like a portrait-painter
who comes suddenly upon an old friend, or upon
an old servant of the family.

We speak of the waiter properly and generally
so called,—the representative of the whole, real,
official race,—and not of the humourist or other
eccentric genius occasionally to be found in it,—
moving out of the orbit of tranquil but fiery waiting,—not absorbed,—not devout towards us,—not
silent or monosyllabical ;—fellows that affect a
character beyond that of waiter, and get spoiled in
club-rooms, and places of theatrical resort.

Your thorough waiter has no ideas out of the
sphere of his duty and the business ; and yet he is
not narrow-minded either. He sees too much
variety of character for that, and has to exercise too
much consideration for the "drunken gentleman."
But his world is the tavern, and all mankind but
its visitors. His female sex are the maid-servants
and his young mistress, or the widow. If he is
ambitious, he aspires to marry one of the latter : if
otherwise, and Molly is prudent, he does not know
but he may carry her off some day to be mistress
of the Golden Lion at Chinksford, where he will
"show off" in the eyes of Betty Laxon who
refused him. He has no feeling of noise itself but
as the sound of dining, or of silence but as a thing
before dinner. Even a loaf with him is hardly a

loaf; it is so many "breads." His longest speech
is the making out of a bill *viva voce*—"Two beefs
—one potatoes—three ales—two wines—six and
twopence"—which he does with an indifferent
celerity, amusing to new-comers who have been re-
lishing their fare, and not considering it as a mere
set of items. He attributes all virtues to everybody, provided they are civil and liberal; and of
the existence of some vices he has no notion.
Gluttony, for instance, with him, is not only in-
conceivable, but looks very like a virtue. He sees
in it only so many more "beefs," and a generous
scorn of the bill. As to wine, or almost any other
liquor, it is out of your power to astonish him with
the quantity you call for. His "Yes, Sir" is as
swift, indifferent, and official, at the fifth bottle as
at the first. Reform and other public events he
looks upon purely as things in the newspaper, and
the newspaper as a thing taken in at taverns, for
gentlemen to read. His own reading is confined
to "Accidents and Offences," and the advertise-
ments for Butlers, which latter he peruses with an
admiring fear, not choosing to give up "a certainty." When young, he was always in a hurry,
and exasperated his mistress by running against
the other waiters, and breaking the "neguses."
As he gets older, he learns to unite swiftness with
caution; declines wasting his breath in immediate
answers to calls; and knows, with a slight turn of
his face, and elevation of his voice, into what precise corner of the room to pitch his "Coming,
Sir." If you told him that, in Shakespeare's time,
waiters said "Anon, anon, Sir," he would be

astonished at the repetition of the same word in one answer, and at the use of three words instead of two ; and he would justly infer, that London could not have been so large, nor the chop-houses so busy, in those days. He would drop one of the two syllables of his "Yes, Sir," if he could ; but business and civility will not allow it ; and therefore he does what he can by running them together in the swift sufficiency of his "Yezzir."

"Thomas ! "

"Yezzir."

"Is my steak coming ? "

"Yezzir."

"And the pint of port ? "

"Yezzir."

"You'll not forget the postman ? "

"Yezzir."

For in the habit of his acquiescence Thomas not seldom says "Yes, Sir," for "No, Sir," the habit itself rendering him intelligible.

His morning dress is a waistcoat or jacket; his coat is for afternoons. If the establishment is flourishing, he likes to get into black as he grows elderly; by which time also he is generally a little corpulent, and wears hair-powder, dressing somewhat laxly about the waist, for convenience of movement. Not however that he draws much upon that part of his body, except as a poise to what he carries; for you may observe that a waiter, in walking, uses only his lowest limbs, from his knees downwards. The movement of all the rest of him is negative, and modified solely by what he bears in his hands. At this period he has

a little money in the funds, and his nieces look up
to him.  He still carries however a napkin under
his arm, as well as a corkscrew in his pocket ; nor,
for all his long habit, can he help feeling a satisfaction at the noise he makes in drawing a cork.
He thinks that no man can do it better; and that
Mr. Smith, who understands wine, is thinking so
too, though he does not take his eyes off the plate.
In his right waistcoat pocket is a snuff-box, with
which he supplies gentlemen late at night, after the
shops are shut up, and when they are in desperate
want of another fillip to their sensations, after the
devil and toasted cheese.  If particularly required,
he will laugh at a joke, especially at that time of
night, justly thinking that gentlemen towards one
in the morning *"will* be facetious."  He is of
opinion it is in " human nature " to be a little fresh
at that period, and to want to be put into a coach.

He announces his acquisition of property by a
bunch of seals to his watch, and perhaps rings on
his fingers ; one of them a mourning ring left him
by his late master, the other a present, either from
his nieces' father, or from some ultra-goodnatured
old gentleman whom he helped into a coach one
night, and who had no silver about him.

To see him dine, somehow, hardly seems
natural.  And he appears to do it as if he had no
right.  You catch him at his dinner in a corner,—
huddled apart,—" Thomas dining ! " instead of
helping dinner.  One fancies that the stewed and
hot meats and the constant smoke ought to be too
much for him, and that he should have neither
appetite nor time for such a meal.

Once a year (for he has few holidays) a couple
of pedestrians meet him on a Sunday in the fields,
and cannot conceive for the life of them who it is;
till the startling recollection occurs—" Good God!
It's the waiter at the Grogram ! "

## SEAMEN  ON  SHORE.

["Indicator," March 15th, 1820.  "Indicator and Companion," 1834.  "Tale for a Chimney Corner," 1869.  A.
Symons, 1888.  C. Kent, 1889.]

THE sole business of a seaman on shore,
who has to go to sea again, is to take
as much pleasure as he can.  The
moment he sets his foot on dry ground,
he turns his back on all salt beef and other salt-
water restrictions.  His long absence, and the
impossibility of getting land pleasures at sea, put
him upon a sort of desperate appetite.  He lands,
like a conqueror taking possession.  He has been
debarred so long, that he is resolved to have that
matter out with the inhabitants.  They must
render an account to him of their treasures, their
women, their victualling-stores, their entertain-
ments, their everything; and in return he will
behave like a gentleman, and scatter his gold.

And first of the common sailor.  The moment
the common sailor lands, he goes to see the watch-
maker or the old boy at the " Ship."

*Reader.* What, sir !  Before his mistress ?

*Indicator.* Excuse me, madam, his mistress,
christened Elizabeth Monson, but more familiarly

known by the appellation of Bet Monson, has been
with him already.   You remember the ballad—

When black-eyed Susan came on board, &c.

The first object of the seaman on landing is to
spend his money, but his first sensation on landing
is the strange firmness of the earth, which he goes
treading in a sort of heavy light way, half waggoner
and half dancing-master, his shoulders rolling, and
his feet touching and going; the same way, in
short, in which he keeps himself prepared for all
the rolling chances of the vessel, when on deck.
There is always to us this appearance of lightness
of foot and heavy strength of upper works, in a
sailor.  And he feels it himself.  He lets his jacket
fly open, and his shoulders slouch, and his hair
grow long, to be gathered into a heavy pigtail;
but when full dressed, he prides himself on a certain
gentility of toe, on a white stocking and a *natty*
shoe, issuing lightly out of the flowing blue trouser.
His arms are neutral, hanging and swinging in a
curve aloof; his hands half open, as if they had
just been handling ropes, and had no object in life
but to handle them again.   He is proud of appearing in a new hat and slops, with a Belcher hand
kerchief flowing loosely round his neck, and the
corner of another out of his pocket.  Thus equipped,
with pinchbeck buckles in his shoes (which he
bought for gold), he puts some tobacco in his
mouth, not as if he were going to use it directly,
but as if he stuffed it in a pouch on one side, as a
pelican does fish, to employ it hereafter; and so,
with Bet Monson at his side, and perhaps a cane or

whanghee twisted under his other arm, sallies forth
to take possession of all Lubberland. He buys everything that he comes athwart—nuts, gingerbread,
apples, shoe-strings, beer, brandy, gin, buckles,
knives, a watch (two, if he has money enough),
gowns and handkerchiefs for Bet and his mother
and sisters, dozens of "Superfine Best Men's
Cotton Stockings," dozens of "Superfine Best
Women's Cotton Ditto," best good Check for
Shirts (though he has too much already), infinite
needles and thread (to sew his trousers with some
day), a footman's laced hat, bear's grease, to make
his hair grow (by way of joke), several sticks, all
sorts of Jew articles, a flute (which he can't play,
and never intends), a leg of mutton, which he
carries somewhere to roast, and for a piece of
which the landlord of the " Ship " makes him pay
twice what he gave for the whole ; in short, all
that money can be spent upon, which is everything
but medicine gratis, and this he would insist on
paying for. He would buy all the painted parrots
on an Italian's head, on purpose to break them,
rather than not spend his money. He has fiddles
and a dance at the " Ship," with oceans of flip and
grog ; and gives the blind fiddler tobacco for
sweetmeats, and half-a-crown for treading on his
toe. He asks the landlady, with a sigh, after her
daughter Nanse, who first fired his heart with her
silk stockings ; and finding that she is married and
in trouble, leaves five crowns for her, which the
old lady appropriates as part payment for a shilling
in advance. He goes to the Port playhouse with
Bet Monson, and a great red handkerchief full of

apples, gingerbread nuts, and fresh beef; calls out for the fiddlers and "Rule Britannia;" pelts Tom Sikes in the pit; and compares Othello to the black ship's-cook in his white nightcap. When he comes to London, he and some messmates take a hackney-coach, full of Bet Monsons and tobacco-pipes, and go through the streets smoking and lolling out of window. He has ever been cautious of venturing on horseback, and among his other sights in foreign parts, relates with unfeigned astonishment how he has seen the Turks ride: "Only," says he, guarding against the hearer's incredulity, "they have saddle-boxes to hold 'em in, fore and aft, and shovels like for stirrups." He will tell you how the Chinese drink, and the *Negurs* dance, and the monkeys pelt you with cocoa-nuts; and how King Domy would have built him a mud hut and made him a peer of the realm, if he would have stopped with him, and taught him to make trousers. He has a sister at a "School for Young Ladies," who blushes with a mixture of pleasure and shame at his appearance; and whose confusion he completes by slipping fourpence into her hand, and saying out loud that he has "no more copper" about him. His mother and elder sisters at home doat on all he says and does; telling him, however, that he is a great sea fellow, and was always wild ever since he was a hop-o'-my-thumb, no higher than the window locker. He tells his mother that she would be a duchess in Paranaboo; at which the good old portly dame laughs and looks proud. When his sisters complain of his romping, he says that they are only sorry it is not the baker. He

frightens them with a mask made after the New
Zealand fashion, and is forgiven for his learning.
Their mantelpiece is filled by him with shells and
shark's teeth ; and when he goes to sea again,
there is no end of tears, and " God bless you's ! "
and home-made gingerbread.　　　　　　　.

His Officer on shore does much of all this, only,
generally speaking, in a higher taste.　The moment he lands, he buys quantities of jewellery and
other valuables, for all the females of his acquaintance ; and is taken in for every article.　He sends
in a cartload of fresh meat to the ship, though he
is going to town next day; and calling in at a
chandler's for some candles, is persuaded to buy a
dozen of green wax, with which he lights up the
ship at evening ; regretting that the fine moonlight
hinders the effect of the colour.　A man, with a
bundle beneath his arm, accosts him in an under-
tone ; and, with a look in which respect for his
knowledge is mixed with an avowed zeal for his
own interest, asks if his Honour will just step
under the gangway here,. and inspect some real
India shawls.　The gallant Lieutenant says to himself, " This fellow knows what's what, by his face ; "
and so he proves it, by being taken in on the spot.
When he brings the shawls home, he says to his
sister with an air of triumph, " There, Poll, there's
something for you ; only cost me twelve, and is
worth twenty if it's worth a dollar."　She turns
pale—" Twenty what, my dear George ? Why,
you haven't given twelve dollars for it, I hope ? "
" Not I, by the Lord."—" That's lucky ; because
you see, my dear George, that all together is not

worth more than fourteen or fifteen shillings."
"Fourteen or fifteen what ! Why it's real India,
en't it ? Why the fellow told me so ; or I'm sure
I'd as soon "—(here he tries to hide his blushes
with a bluster)—" I'd as soon have given him
twelve douses on the chaps as twelve guineas."—
"Twelve *guineas !* " exclaims the sister ; and
then drawling forth, "Why—my—*dear*—George,"
is proceeding to show him what the articles would
have cost at Condell's, when he interrupts her by
requesting her to go and choose for herself a tea-
table service. He then makes his escape to some
messmates at a coffee-house, and drowns his recollection of the shawls in the best wine, and a
discussion on the comparative merits of the English
and West-Indian beauties and tables. At the
theatre afterwards, where he has never been before,
he takes a lady at the back of one of the boxes for
a woman of quality ; and when, after returning his
long respectful gaze with a smile, she turns aside
and puts her handkerchief to her mouth, he thinks
it is in derision, till his friend undeceives him. He
is introduced to the lady ; and ever afterwards, at
first sight of a woman of quality (without any disparagement either to those charming personages),
expects her to give him a smile. He thinks the
other ladies much better creatures than they are
taken for ; and for their parts, they tell him, that
if all men were like himself, they would trust the
sex again :—which, for aught we know, is the
truth. He has, indeed, what he thinks a very
liberal opinion of ladies in general ; judging them
all, in a manner, with the eye of a seaman's expe-

rience. Yet he will believe nevertheless in the
"true-love" of any given damsel whom he seeks
in the way of marriage, let him roam as much, or
remain as long at a distance, as he pleases. It is
not that he wants feeling ; but that he has read of
it, time out of mind, in songs ; and he looks upon
constancy as a sort of exploit, answering to those
which he performs at sea. He is nice in his watches
and linen. He makes you presents of cornelians,
antique seals, cocoa-nuts set in silver, and other
valuables. When he shakes hands with you, it is
like being caught in a windlass. He would not
swagger about the streets in his uniform, for the
world. He is generally modest in company, though
liable to be irritated by what he thinks ungentle-
manly behaviour. - He is also liable to be rendered
irritable by sickness ; partly because he has been
used to command others, and to be served with all
possible deference and alacrity ; and partly, because the idea of suffering pain, without any honour
or profit to get by it, is unprofessional, and he is
not accustomed to it. He treats talents unlike his
own with great respect. He often perceives his
own so little felt, that it teaches him this feeling
for that of others. Besides, he admires the quantity of information which people can get, without
travelling like himself ; especially when he sees
how interesting his own becomes, to them as well
as to everybody else. When he tells a story, particularly if full of wonders, he takes care to maintain his character for truth and simplicity, by
qualifying it with all possible reservations, conces-
sions, and anticipations of objection ; such as, "in

case, at such times as, so to speak, as it were, at
least, at any rate." He seldom uses sea-terms but
when jocosely provoked by something contrary to
his habits of life ; as for instance, if he is always
meeting you on horseback, he asks if you never
mean to walk the deck again ; or if he finds you
studying day after day, he says you are always
overhauling your log-book. He makes more new
acquaintances, and forgets his old ones less, than
any other man in the busy world ; for he is so
compelled to make his home everywhere, remem-
bers his native one as such a place of enjoyment,
has all his friendly recollections so fixed upon his
mind at sea, and has so much to tell and to hear
when he returns, that change and separation lose
with him the most heartless part of their nature.
He also sees such a variety of customs and manners,
that he becomes charitable in his opinions altogether ; and charity, while it diffuses the affections,
cannot let the old ones go. Half the secret of
human intercourse is to make allowance for each
other.

When the Officer is superannuated or retires, he
becomes, if intelligent and inquiring, one of the
most agreeable old men in the world, equally welcome to the silent for his card-playing, and to the
conversational for his recollections. He is fond of
astronomy and books of voyages, and is immortal
with all who know him for having been round the
world, or seen the transit of Venus, or had one of
his fingers carried off by a New Zealand hatchet,
or a present of feathers from an Otaheitan beauty.
If not elevated by his acquirements above some of

his humbler tastes, he delights in a corner-cupboard holding his cocoa-nuts and punch-bowl ; has his summer-house castellated and planted with wooden cannon ; and sets up the figure of his old ship, the " Britannia " or the " Lovely Nancy," for a statue in the garden ; where it stares eternally with red cheeks and round black eyes, as if in astonishment at its situation.

Chaucer, who wrote his " Canterbury Tales " about four hundred and thirty years ago, has among his other characters in that work a SHIP-MAN, who is exactly of the same cast as the modern sailor,—the same robustness, courage, and rough-drawn virtue, doing its duty, without being very nice in helping itself to its recreations. There is the very dirk, the complexion, the jollity, the experience, and the bad horsemanship. The plain unaffected ending of the description has the air of a sailor's own speech ; while the line about the beard is exceedingly picturesque, poetical, and comprehensive. In copying it out, we shall merely alter the old spelling, where the words are still modern.

> A shipman was there, wonned far by west ;
> For aught I wot, he was of Dartëmouth.
> He rode opon a rouncie, as he couth,[1]
> All in a gown of falding to the knee.
> A dagger hanging by a lace had he,
> About his neck, under his arm adown :
> The hot summer had made his hew all brown :
> And certainly he was a good felaw.
> Full many a draught of wine he haddë draw
> From Bourdeaux ward, while that the chapman slep.

[1] He rode upon a hack-horse, as well as he could.

Of nice conscience took he no keep.
If that he fought and had the higher hand, ˗
By water he sent 'em home to every land.
But of his craft, to reckon well his tides,
His streamës and his strandës him besides,
His harborough, his moon, and his lode manage,
There was not such from Hull unto Carthage.
Hardy he was, and wise, I undertake;
With many a tempest had his beard been shake.
He knew well all the havens, as they were,
From Gothland to the Cape de Finisterre,
And every creek in Briton and in Spain.
His barge ycleped was the Magdelain.

When about to tell his Tale, he tells his fellow-travellers that he shall clink them so merry a bell,

That it shall waken all this company:
But it shall not be of philosophy,
Nor of physick, nor of terms quaint of law;
There is but little Latin in my maw.

The story he tells is a well-known one in the Italian novels, of a monk who made love to a merchant's wife, and borrowed a hundred francs of the husband to give her. She accordingly admits his addresses during the absence of her good man on a journey. When the latter returns, he applies to the cunning monk for repayment, and is referred to the lady; who thus finds her mercenary behaviour outwitted.[1]

[1] "The common sailor was a son of my nurse at school, and the officer a connection of my own by marriage."— "Autobiography," p. 250.
Cf. the following paragraph about sailors (from "Critical Essays on the Performers of the London Theatres"):—"Mr. Bannister possesses all the firmness with all the good-

## COACHES.

[" Indicator," Aug. 23rd and 30th, 1820.  " Indicator and
Companion," 1834.   " Tale for Chimney Corner," 1869.
C. Kent, 1889.]

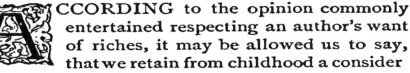CCORDING to the opinion commonly
entertained respecting an author's want
of riches, it may be allowed us to say,
that we retain from childhood a consider
able notion of "a ride in a coach."   Nor do we
hesitate to confess, that by coach, we especially
mean a hired one ; from the equivocal rank of the
post-chaise, down to that despised old cast-away,
the hackney.

It is true, that the carriage, as it is indifferently
called (as if nothing less genteel could carry any
one) is a more decided thing than the chaise ; it
may be swifter even than the mail, leaves the stage
at a still greater distance in every respect, and
(forgetting what it may come to itself) darts by the
poor old lumbering hackney with immeasurable
contempt.   It rolls with a prouder ease than any
other vehicle.   It is full of cushions and comfort ;
elegantly coloured inside and out; rich, yet neat ;
light and rapid, yet substantial.   The horses seem

nature of the seaman ; his open smile, his sincere tone
of voice, his careless gait, his person that seems to have
undergone all that long and robust labour that must earn
the sailor a day of jollity ; in short, every action of his body
and his mind belongs to that generous race, of whom Charles
the Second observed, they 'got their money like horses and
spent it like asses.' "—ED.

proud to draw it. The fat and fair-wigged coachman "lends his sounding lash," his arm only in action and that but little, his body well set with its own weight. The footman, in the pride of his nonchalance, holding by the straps behind, and glancing down sideways betwixt his cocked-hat and neckcloth, stands swinging from east to west upon his springy toes. The horses rush along amidst their glancing harness. Spotted dogs leap about them, barking with a princely superfluity of noise. The hammer-cloth trembles through all its fringe.— The paint flashes in the sun. We, contemptuous of everything less convenient, bow backwards and forwards with a certain indifferent air of gentility, infinitely predominant. Suddenly, with a happy mixture of turbulence and truth, the carriage dashes up by the curb-stone to the very point desired, and stops with a lordly wilfulness of decision. The coachman looks as if nothing had happened. The footman is down in an instant; the knocker reverberates into the farthest corner of the house; doors, both carriage and house, are open;—we descend, casting a matter-of-course eye at the by-standers; and the moment we touch the pavement, the vehicle, as if conscious of what it has carried, and relieved from the weight of our importance, recovers from its sidelong inclination with a jerk, tossing and panting, as it were, for very breath, like the proud heads of the horses.

All this, it must be owned, is very pretty; but it is also gouty and superfluous. It is too convenient,—too exacting,—too exclusive. We must

I.                                                    G

get too much for it, and lose too much by it.    Its
plenty, as Ovid says, makes us poor.    We neither
have it in the republic of letters, nor would desire
it in any less Jacobinical state.    Horses, as many
as you please, provided men have enough to eat;—
hired coaches, a reasonable number:—but health
and good-humour at all events.

Gigs and curricles are things less objectionable,
because they cannot be so relied upon as substi-
tutes for exercise.    Our taste in them, we must confess, is not genuine.    How shall we own it?    We
like to be driven, instead of drive;—to read or
look about us, instead of keeping watch on a
horse's head.    We have no relish even for vehicles
of this description that are not safe.    Danger is a
good thing for giving a fillip to a man's ideas; but
even danger, to us, must come recommended by
something useful.    We have no ambition to have
TANDEM written on our tombstone.

The prettiest of these vehicles undoubtedly is
the curricle, which is also the safest.    There is
something worth looking at in the pair of horses,
with that sparkling pole of steel laid across them.
It is like a bar of music, comprising their harmonious course.    But to us, even gigs are but a sort
of unsuccessful run at gentility.    The driver, to all
intents and purposes, had better be on the horse.
Horseback is the noblest way of being carried in
the world.    It is cheaper than any other mode of
riding; it is common to all ranks; and it is manly,
graceful, and healthy.    The handsomest mixture
of danger with dignity, in the shape of a carriage,
was the tall phaeton with its yellow wings.    We

remember looking up to it with respect in our
childhood, partly for its own loftiness, partly for
its name, and perhaps for the figure it makes in the
prints to novels of that period. The most gallant
figure which mere modern driving ever cut, was in
the person of a late Duke of Hamilton; of whom
we have read or heard somewhere, that he used to
dash round the streets of Rome, with his horses
panting, and his hounds barking about his phaeton,
to the equal fright and admiration of the Masters
of the World, who were accustomed to witness
nothing higher than a lumbering old coach, or a
cardinal on a mule.

A post-chaise involves the idea of travelling,
which in the company of those we love is home in
motion. The smooth running along the road, the
fresh air, the variety of scene, the leafy roads, the
bursting prospects, the clatter through a town, the
gaping gaze of a village, the hearty appetite, the
leisure (your chaise waiting only upon your own
movements), even the little contradictions to
home-comfort, and the expedients upon which they
set us, all put the animal spirits at work, and
throw a novelty over the road of life. If anything
could grind us young again, it would be the wheels
of a post-chaise. The only monotonous sight is
the perpetual up-and-down movement of the postilion, who, we wish exceedingly, could take a
chair. His occasional retreat to the bar which
occupies the place of a box, and his affecting to sit
upon it, only remind us of its exquisite want of
accommodation. But some have given the bar,
lately, a surreptitious squeeze in the middle, and

flattened it a little into something obliquely resembling an inconvenient seat.

If we are to believe the merry Columbus of Down-Hall, calashes, now almost obsolete for any purpose, used to be hired for travelling occasions a hundred years back; but he preferred a chariot; and neither was good. Yet see how pleasantly good-humour rides over its inconveniences.

Then answer'd 'Squire Morley, "Pray get a calash,
That in summer may burn, and in winter may splash;
I love dirt and dust; and 'tis always my pleasure
To take with me much of the soil that I measure."

But Matthew thought better; for Matthew thought right,
And hired a chariot so trim and so tight,
That extremes both of winter and summer might pass;
For one window was canvas, the other was glass.

"Draw up," quoth friend Matthew; "Pull down," quoth friend John;
"We shall be both hotter and colder anon."
Thus, talking and scolding, they forward did speed;
And Ralpho paced by under Newman the Swede.

Into an old inn did this equipage roll,
At a town they call Hodson, the sign of the Bull;
Near a nymph with an urn that divides the highway,
And into a puddle throws mother of tea.

"Come here, my sweet landlady, pray how d'ye do?
Where is Cicely so cleanly, and Prudence, and Sue?
And where is the widow that dwelt here below?
And the ostler that sung about eight years ago?

And where is your sister, so mild and so dear,
Whose voice to her maids like a trumpet was clear?"
"By my troth," she replies, "you grow younger, I think;
And pray, Sir, what wine does the gentleman drink?

"Why now let me die, Sir, or live upon trust,
If I know to which question to answer you first:

Why, things, since I saw you, most strangely have varied ;
The ostler is hang'd, and the widow is married.

"And Prue left a child for the parish to nurse,
And Cicely went off with a gentleman's purse ;
And as to my sister, so mild and so dear,
She has lain in the church-yard full many a year."

"Well ; peace to her ashes ! What signifies grief?
She roasted red veal, and she powder'd lean beef :
Full nicely she knew to cook up a fine dish ;
For tough were her pullets, and tender her fish."

PRIOR.

This quotation reminds us of a little poem by
the same author, entitled the "Secretary," which,
as it is short, and runs upon chaise-wheels, and
seems to have slipped the notice it deserves, we
will do ourselves the pleasure of extracting also.
It was written when he was Secretary of Embassy
at the Hague, where he seems to have edified the
Dutch with his insisting upon enjoying himself.
The astonishment with which the good Hollander
and his wife look up to him as he rides, and the
touch of yawning dialect at the end, are extremely
pleasant.

While with labour assiduous due pleasure I mix,
And in one day atone for the business of six,
In a little Dutch chaise on a Saturday night,
On my left hand my Horace, a nymph on my right :
No Memoirs to compose, and no Post-boy to move,
That on Sunday may hinder the softness of love ;
For her, neither visits, nor parties at tea,
Nor the long-winded cant of a dull Refugee :
This night and the next shall be hers, shall be mine,—
To good or ill-fortune the third we resign :
Thus scorning the world and superior to fate,
I drive on my car in processional state.
So with Phia through Athens Pisistratus rode ;

Men thought her Minerva, and him a new god.
But why should I stories of Athens rehearse,
Where people knew love, and were partial to verse?
Since none can with justice my pleasures oppose,
In Holland half drowned in interest and prose?
By Greece and past ages what need I be tried,
When the Hague and the present are both on my side?
And is it enough for the joys of the day,
To think what Anacreon or Sappho would say?
When good Vandergoes, and his provident *vrow*,
As they gaze on my triumph, do freely allow,
That, search all the province, you'll find no man *dàr* is
So blest as the *Englishen Heer Secretar'* is.

If Prior had been living now, he would have found the want of travelling accommodation flourishing most in a country for whose graver wants we have to answer, without having her wit to help us. There is a story told of an Irish post-chaise, the occupier of which, without quitting it, had to take to his heels. It was going down hill as fast as wind and the impossibility of stopping could make it, when the foot passengers observed a couple of legs underneath, emulating with all their might the rapidity of the wheels. The bottom had come out; and the gentleman was obliged to run for his life.

We must relate another anecdote of an Irish post-chaise, merely to show the natural tendencies of the people to be lawless in self-defence. A friend of ours,[1] who was travelling among them, used to have this proposition put to him by the postilion whenever he approached a turnpike. "Plase your honour, will I drive at the pike?" The pike hung loosely across the road. Luckily, the rider happened to be of as lawless a turn for

[1] Mr. Shelley.

justice as the driver, so the answer was always a
cordial one :—" Oh yes—drive at the pike." The
pike made way accordingly ; and in a minute or
two, the gate people were heard and seen, screaming in vain after the illegal charioteers.

> **Fertur equis auriga, neque audit currus.**
> VIRGIL.

> The driver 's borne beyond their swearing,
> And the post-chaise is hard of hearing.

As to following them, nobody in Ireland thinks
of moving too much, legal or illegal.

The pleasure to be had in a mail-coach is not
so much at one's command, as that in a post-chaise.
There is generally too little room in it, and too
much hurry out of it. The company must not
lounge over their breakfast, even if they are all
agreed. It is an understood thing, that they are to
be uncomfortably punctual. They must get in at
seven o'clock, though they are all going upon
business they do not like or care about, or will have
to wait till nine before they can do any thing.
Some persons know how to manage this haste,
and breakfast and dine in the cracking of a whip.
They stick with their fork, they joint, they sliver,
they bolt. Legs and wings vanish before them
like a dragon's before a knight-errant. But if one
is not a clergyman or a regular jolly fellow, one
has no chance this way. To be diffident or polite,
is fatal. It is a merit eagerly acknowledged, and as
quickly set aside. At last you begin upon a leg,
and are called off.

A very troublesome degree of science is neces-

sary for being well settled in the coach. We remember travelling in our youth, upon the north
road, with an orthodox elderly gentleman of venerable peruke, who talked much with a grave-look-
ing young man about universities, and won our
inexperienced heart with a notion that he was deep
in Horace and Virgil. He was much deeper in
his wig. Towards evening, as he seemed restless,
we asked with much diffidence whether a change,
even for the worse, might not relieve him ; for we
were riding backwards, and thought all elderly
people disliked that way. He insinuated the very
objection ; so we recoiled from asking him again.
In a minute or two, however, he insisted that we
were uneasy ourselves, and that he must relieve us
for our own sake. We protested as filially as
possible against this ; but at last, out of mere shame
of disputing the point with so benevolent an elder,
we changed seats with him. After an interval of
bland meditation we found the evening sun full in
our face.—His new comfort set him dozing ; and
every now and then he jerked his wig in our eyes,
till we had the pleasure to see him take out a
nightcap and look extremely ghastly.—The same
person, and his serious young companion, tricked
us out of a good bed we happened to get at the inn.

The greatest peculiarity attending a mail-coach
arises from its travelling at night. The gradual
decline of talk, the incipient snore, the rustling
and alteration of legs and nightcaps, the cessation
of other noises on the road—the sound of the wind
or rain, of the moist circuit of the wheels, and of
the time-beating tread of the horses—all dispose

the traveller, who cannot sleep, to a double sense
of the little that is left him to observe. The coach
stops, the door opens, a rush of cold air announces
at once the demands and merits of the guard, who
is taking his leave, and is anxious to remember us.
The door is clapped to again ; the sound of everything outside becomes dim ; and voices are heard
knocking up the people of the inn, and answered
by issuing yawns and excuses. Wooden shoes
clog heavily about. The horses' mouths are heard
swilling up the water out of tubs. All is still
again, and some one in the coach takes a long
breath. The driver mounts, and we resume our
way. It happens that we can sleep anywhere except
in a mail-coach ; so that we hate to see a prudent,
warm, old fellow, who has been eating our fowls
and intercepting our toast, put on his nightcap in
order to settle himself till morning. We rejoice in
the digs that his neighbour's elbow gives him, and
hail the long-legged traveller that sits opposite. A
passenger of our wakeful description must try to
content himself with listening to the sounds above
mentioned ; or thinking of his friends ; or turning
verses, as Sir Richard Blackmore did, "to the
rumbling of his coach's wheels," or chatting with
the servant-girl who is going to place (may nobody
get her dismissed nine months hence !) or protecting her against the Methodist in the corner ; or if
alone with her, and she has a kind face, protecting
her against a much more difficult person—himself.
Really we must say that enough credit is not given
to us lawless persons who say all we think, and
would have the world enjoy all it could. There is

the author of the "Mail-coach Adventure," for instance.     With all his amorous verses, his yearnings after the pleasant laws of the Golden Age, and even his very hymns (which, we confess, are a little mystic), we would rather trust a fair traveller to his keeping, than some much graver writers we have heard of.     If he forgot himself, he would not think it a part of virtue to forget her.     But his absolution is not ready at hand, as for graver sinners.     The very intensity of the sense of pleasure will often keep a man from destroying its after-thoughts in another ; when harsher systems will forget themselves, only to confound brutality with repentance.

The stage-coach is a very great and unpretending accommodation.     It is a cheap substitute, notwithstanding all its eighteen-penny and two-and-sixpenny temptations, for keeping a carriage or a horse ; and we really think, in spite of its gossiping, is no mean help to village liberality ; for its passengers are so mixed, so often varied, so little yet so much together, so compelled to accommodate, so willing to pass a short time pleasantly, and so liable to the criticism of strangers, that it is hard if they do not get a habit of speaking, or even thinking more kindly of one another than if they mingled less often, or under other circumstances. The old and infirm are treated with reverence ; the ailing sympathized with ; the healthy congratulated ; the rich not distinguished ; the poor well met : the young, with their faces conscious of ride, patronised, and allowed to be extra.     Even the fiery, nay the fat, learn to bear with each other ; and if some high thoughted persons will talk now and then of their great acquaintances, or their preference of a carriage, there is an instinct which tells the rest, that they would not make such appeals to their good opinion, if they valued it so little as might be supposed. Stoppings and dust are not pleasant, but the latter may be had on much grander occasions ; and if any one is so unlucky as never to keep another stopping himself, he must be content with the superiority of his virtue.

The mail or stage-coachman, upon the whole, is no inhuman mass of great-coat, gruffness, civility, and old boots. The latter is the politer, from the smaller range of acquaintance, and his necessity for preserving them. His face is red, and his voice rough, by the same process of drink and catarrh. He has a silver watch with a steel chain, and plenty of loose silver in his pocket, mixed with halfpence. He serves the houses he goes by for a clock. He takes a glass at every alehouse ; for thirst, when it is dry, and for warmth when it is wet. He likes to show the judicious reach of his whip, by twigging a dog or a goose on the road, or children that get in the way. His tenderness to descending old ladies is particular. He touches his hat to Mr. Smith. He gives "the young woman" a ride, and lends her his box-coat in the rain. His liberality in imparting his knowledge to any one that has the good fortune to ride on the box with him, is a happy mixture of deference, conscious possession, and familiarity. His information chiefly lies in the occupancy of houses on the road, prize-fighters, Bow-street runners, and accidents. He concludes that you know Dick Sams, or Old Joey, and proceeds to relate some of the stories that relish his pot and tobacco in the evening. If any of the four-in-hand gentry go by, he shakes his head, and thinks they might find something better to do. His contempt for them is founded on modesty. He tells you that his off-hand horse is as pretty a goer as ever was, but that Kitty—"Yeah, now there, Kitty, can't you be still? Kitty's a devil, Sir, for all you wouldn't think it." He knows that the boys on the road admire him, and gives the horses an indifferent lash with his whip as they go by. If you wish to know what rain and dust can do, you should look at his old hat. There is an indescribably placid and paternal look in the position of his corduroy knees and old top-boots on the foot-board, with their pointed toes and never-cleaned soles. His *beau idéal* of appearance is a frock-coat, with mother-o'-pearl buttons, a striped yellow waistcoat, and a flower in his mouth.

> But all our praises why for Charles and Robert?
> Rise, honest Mews, and sing the classic Bobart.

Is the quadrijugal virtue of that learned person still extant? That Olympic and Baccalaureated charioteer?—That best educated and most erudite of coachmen, of whom Dominie Sampson is alone worthy to speak? That singular punning and driving commentary on the *Sunt quos curriculo collegisse?* In short, the worthy and agreeable Mr. Bobart,[1] Bachelor of Arts, who drove the Oxford stage some years ago, capped verses and the

---

[1] See also the "Autobiography," p. 99, for further particulars of Mr. B——.—Ed.

front of his hat with equal dexterity, and read
Horace over his brandy-and-water of an evening?
We had once the pleasure of being beaten by him
in that capital art, he having brought up against us
an unusual number of those cross-armed letters, as
puzzling to verse-cappers as iron-cats unto cavalry,
ycleped X's; which said warfare he was pleased
to call to mind in after-times, unto divers of our
comrades. The modest and natural greatness with
which he used to say "Yait," to his horses, and
then turn round with his rosy gills, and an eye
like a fish, and give out the required verse, can
never pass away from us, as long as verses or
horses run.

Of the hackney-coach we cannot make as short
work, as many persons like to make of it in
reality. Perhaps it is partly a sense of the contempt it undergoes, which induces us to endeavour
to make the best of it. But it has its merits, as we
shall show presently. In the account of its de-
merits, we have been anticipated by a new, and
we are sorry to say a very good, poetess, of the
name of Lucy V—— L——, who has favoured us
with a sight of a manuscript poem,[1] in which they
are related with great nicety and sensitiveness.

*Reader.* What, Sir, sorry to say that a lady is a
good poetess?

*Indicator.* Only inasmuch, Madam, as the lady
gives such authority to the anti-social view of this
subject, and will not agree with us as to the beatitude of the hackney-coach.—But hold':—upon

---

[1] By Mr. Keats. The manuscript purports to have bee
written by a Miss Lucy Vaughan Lloyd.

turning to the manuscript again, we find that the
objections are put into the mouth of a dandy courtier. This makes a great difference. The hackney
resumes all which it had lost in the good graces of
the fair authoress. The only wonder is, how the
courtier could talk so well. Here is the passage.

Eban, untempted by the Pastry-cooks,
(Of Pastry he got store within the Palace,)
With hasty steps, wrapp'd cloak, and solemn looks,
Incognito upon his errand sallies,
His smelling-bottle ready for the alleys ;
He pass'd the Hurdy-gurdies with disdain,
Vowing he'd have them sent on board the galleys :
Just as he made his vow, it 'gan to rain,
Therefore he call'd a coach, and bade it drive amain.

" I'll pull the string," said he, and further said,
"Polluted Jarvey !  Ah, thou filthy hack !
Whose strings of life are all dried up and dead,
Whose linsey-wolsey lining hangs all slack,
Whose rug is straw, whose wholeness is a crack ;
And evermore thy steps go clatter-clitter ;
Whose glass once up can never be got back,
Who prov'st, with jolting arguments and bitter,
That 'tis of vile no-use to travel in a litter.

"Thou inconvenience ! thou hungry crop
For all corn ! thou snail creeper to and fro,
Who while thou goest ever seem'st to stop,
And fiddle-faddle standest while you go ;
I' the morning, freighted with a weight of woe,
Unto some Lazar-house thou journiest,
And in the evening tak'st a double row
Of dowdies, for some dance or party drest,
Besides the goods meanwhile thou movest east and west.

" By thy ungallant bearing and sad mien,
An inch appears the utmost thou couldst budge ;
Yet at the slightest nod, or hint, or sign,
Round to the curb-stone patient dost thou trudge,

School'd in a beckon, learned in a nudge ;
A dull-eyed Argus watching for a fare ;
Quiet and plodding, thou dost bear no grudge
To whisking Tilburies or Phaetons rare,
Curricles, or Mail-coaches, swift beyond compare."

Philosophizing thus, he pull'd the check,
And bade the coachman wheel to such a street ;
Who turning much his body, more his neck,
Louted full low, and hoarsely did him greet.

The tact here is so nice, of the infirmities which are but too likely to beset our poor old friend, that we should only spoil it to say more. To pass then to the merits.

[1] One of the greatest helps to a sense of merit in other things, is a consciousness of one's own wants. Do you despise a hackney-coach? ' Get tired; get old ; get young again. Lay down your carriage, or make it less uneasily too easy. Have to stand up half an hour, out of a storm, under a gateway. Be ill, and wish to visit a friend who is worse. Fall in love, and want to sit next your mistress. Or if all this will not do, fall in a cellar.

Ben Jonson, in a fit of indignation at the niggardliness of James the First, exclaimed, "He despises me, I suppose, because I live in an alley :—tell him his soul lives in an alley." We think we see a hackney-coach moved out of its ordinary patience, and hear it say, "You there, who sit looking so scornfully at me out of your carriage, you are yourself the thing you take me for. Your understanding is a hackney-coach. It is lumbering, rickety, and at a stand. When it

---

[1] The "Indicator," of Aug. 30th, 1820, begins here.

moves, it is drawn by things like itself. It is at once the most stationary and the most servile of common-places. And when a good thing is put into it, it does not know it."

But it is difficult to imagine a hackney-coach under so irritable an aspect. Hogarth has drawn a set of hats or wigs with countenances of their own. We have noticed the same thing in the faces of houses; and it sometimes gets in one's way in a landscape-painting, with the outlines of the massy trees. A friend tells us, that the hackney-coach has its countenance, with gesticulation besides : and now he has pointed it out, we can easily fancy it. Some of them look chucked under the chin, some nodding, some coming at you sideways. We shall never find it easy, however, to fancy the irritable aspect above mentioned. A hackney-coach always appeared to us the most quiescent of moveables. Its horses and it, slumbering on a stand, are an emblem of all the patience in creation, animate and inanimate. The submission with which the coach takes every variety of the weather, dust, rain, and wind, never moving but when some eddying blast makes its old body seem to shiver, is only surpassed by the vital patience of the horses. Can anything better illustrate the poet's line about—

Years that bring the philosophic mind,

than the still-hung head, the dim indifferent eye, the dragged and blunt-cornered mouth, and the gaunt imbecility of body dropping its weight on three tired legs in order to give repose to the lame one ? When it has blinkers on, they seem to be shutting up its eyes for death, like the windows of a house. Fatigue and the habit of suffering have become as natural to the creature as the bit to its mouth. Once in half an hour it moves the position of its leg, or shakes its drooping ears. The whip makes it go, more from habit than from pain. Its coat has become almost callous to minor stings. The blind and staggering fly in autumn might come to die against its cheek.

Of a pair of hackney-coach horses, one so much resembles the other that it seems unnecessary for them to compare notes. They have that within, which is beyond the comparative. They no longer bend their heads towards each other, as they go. They stand together as if unconscious of one another's company, but they are not. An old horse misses his companion, like an old man. The presence of an associate, who has gone through pain and suffering with us, need not say anything. It is talk, and memory, and everything. Something of this it may be to our old friends in harness. What are they thinking of, while they stand motionless in the rain? Do they remember? Do they dream? Do they still, unperplexed as their old blood is by too many foods, receive a pleasure from the elements; a dull refreshment from the air and sun? Have they yet a palate for the hay which they pull so feebly? or for the rarer grain, which induces them to perform their only voluntary gesture of any vivacity, and toss up the bags that are fastened on their mouths, to get at its shallow feast?

1.                                                    H

If the old horse were gifted with memory, (and who shall say he is not, in one thing as well as another?) it might be at once the most melancholy and pleasantest faculty he has; for the commonest hack has very likely been a hunter or racer; has had his days of lustre and enjoyment; has darted along the course, and scoured the pasture; has carried his master proudly, or his lady gently; has pranced, has galloped, has neighed aloud, has dared, has forded, has spurned at mastery, has graced it and made it proud, has rejoiced the eye, has been crowded to as an actor, has been all instinct with life and quickness, has had its very fear admired as courage, and been sat upon by valour as its chosen seat.

> His ears up-pricked; his braided hanging mane
> Upon his compass'd crest now stands on end;
> His nostrils drink the air; and forth again,
> As from a furnace, vapours doth he send;
> > His eye, which glistens scornfully like fire,
> > Shows his hot courage and his high desire.

> Sometimes he trots as if he told the steps,
> With gentle majesty, and modest pride;
> Anon he rears upright, curvets and leaps,
> As who would say, lo! thus my strength is tried,
> > And thus I do to captivate the eye
> > Of the fair breeder that is standing by.

> What recketh he his rider's angry stir,
> His flattering holla, or his *Stand, I say?*
> What cares he now for curb, or pricking spur?
> For rich caparisons, or trappings gay?
> > He sees his love, and nothing else he sees,
> > For nothing else with his proud sight agrees.

> Look, when a painter would surpass the life,
> In limning out a well-proportion'd steed,

His art with nature's workmanship at strife,
As if the dead the living should exceed ;
　　So did this horse excel a common one,
　　In shape, in courage, colour, pace, and bone.

Round-hoof'd, short-jointed, fetlock shag and long,
Broad breast, full eyes, small head, and nostril wide ;
High crest, short ears, straight legs, and passing strong ;
Thin mane, thick tail, broad buttock, tender hide ;
　　Look, what a horse should have, he did not lack,
　　Save a proud rider on so proud a back.

Alas ! his only riders now are the rain and a sordid harness ! The least utterance of the wretchedest voice makes him stop and become a fixture. His loves were in existence at the time the old sign, fifty miles hence, was painted. His nostrils drink nothing but what they cannot help, —the water out of an old tub. Not all the hounds in the world could make his ears attain any eminence. His mane is scratchy and lax, his shape an anatomy, his name a mockery. The same great poet who wrote the triumphal verses for him and his loves, has written their living epitaph :—

　　　　　　. **The poor jades**
Lob down their heads, dropping the hide and hips,
The gum down roping from their pale dead eyes ;
And in their pale dull mouths the gimmal bit
Lies foul with chew'd grass, still and motionless.
　　　　　　　　　*K. Henry V., Act* 1.

There is a song called the "High-mettled Racer," describing the progress of a favourite horse's life, from its time of vigour and glory, down to its furnishing food for the dogs. It is not as good as Shakespeare ; but it will do, to those who are half as kind as he. We defy anybody to read that

song or be in the habit of singing it or hearing it
sung, and treat horses as they are sometimes
treated. So much good may an author do, who is
in earnest, and does not go in a pedantic way to
work. We will not say that Plutarch's good-
natured observation about taking care of one's old
horse did more for that class of retired servants
than all the graver lessons of philosophy. For it is
philosophy which first sets people thinking ; and
then some of them put it in a more popular shape.
But we will venture to say, that Plutarch's observation saved many a steed of antiquity a superfluous
thump; and in this respect, the author of the
"High-mettled Racer" (Mr. Dibdin we believe, no
mean man in his way,) may stand by the side of the
old illustrious biographer. Next to ancient causes,
to the inevitable progress of events, and to the
practical part of Christianity (which persons, the
most accused of irreligion, have preserved like a
glorious infant, through ages of blood and fire,) the
kindliness of modern philosophy is more immediately owing to the great national writers of
Europe, in whose schools we have all been children :—to Voltaire in France, and Shakespeare in
England. Shakespeare, in his time, obliquely
pleaded the cause of the Jew, and got him set on a
common level with humanity. The Jew has since
been not only allowed to be human, but some
have undertaken to show him as the " best good
Christian though he knows it not." We shall not
dispute the title with him, nor with the other wor-
shippers of Mammon, who force him to the same
shrine. We allow, as things go in that quarter,

that the Jew is as great a Christian as his neighbour, and his neighbour as great a Jew as he.
There is neither love nor money lost between
them.  But at all events, the Jew is a man; and
with Shakespeare's assistance, the time has arrived,
when we can afford to acknowledge the horse for a
fellow-creature, and treat him as one.  We may
say for him, upon the same grounds and to the
same purpose, as Shakespeare said for the Israelite,
" Hath not a horse organs, dimensions, senses,
affections, passions ? hurt with the same weapons,
subject to the same diseases, healed by the same
means, warmed and cooled by the same winter and
summer, as a Christian is ? "  Oh—but some are
always at hand to cry out,—it would be effeminate
to think too much of these things !—Alas ! we
have no notion of asking the gentlemen to think
too much of anything.  If they will think at all, it
will be a great gain.  As to effeminacy (if we must
use that ungallant and partial word, for want of a
better,) it is cruelty that is effeminate.  It is selfish-
ness that is effeminate.  Anything is effeminate,
which would get an excitement, or save a proper
and manly trouble, at the undue expense of another.—How does the case stand then between
those who ill-treat their horses, and those who
spare them ?

To return to the coach.  Imagine a fine coach
and pair, which are standing at the door of a house,
in all the pride of their sleek strength and beauty,
converted into what they may both really become,
a hackney, and its old shamblers.  Such is one of
the meditations of the philosophic eighteenpenny

rider. A hackney-coach has often the arms of nobility on it. As we are going to get into it, we catch a glimpse of the faded lustre of an earl's or marquis's coronet, and think how many light or proud hearts have ascended those now ricketty steps. In this coach perhaps an elderly lady once rode to her wedding, a blooming and blushing girl. Her mother and sister were on each side of her; the bridegroom opposite in a blossom-coloured coat. They talk of everything in the world of which they are not thinking. The sister was never prouder of her. The mother with difficulty represses her own pride and tears. The bride, thinking he is looking at her, casts down her eyes, pensive in her joy. The bridegroom is at once the proudest, and the humblest, and the happiest man in the world—For our parts, we sit in a corner, and are in love with the sister. We dream she is going to speak to us in answer to some indifferent question, when a hoarse voice comes in at the front window, and says, "Whereabouts, Sir !"

And grief has consecrated thee, thou reverend dilapidation, as well as joy ! Thou hast carried unwilling, as well as willing hearts ; hearts, that have thought the slowest of thy paces too fast ; faces that have sat back in a corner of thee, to hide their tears from the very thought of being seen. In thee the destitute have been taken to the poorhouse, and the wounded and sick to the hospital ; and many an arm has been round many an insensible waist. Into thee the friend or the lover has hurried, in a passion of tears, to lament his loss.

In thee he has hastened to console the dying or the wretched. In thee the father, or mother, or the older kinswoman, more patient in her years, has taken the little child to the grave, the human jewel that must be parted with.

But joy appears in thee again, like the look-in of the sun-shine. If the lover has gone in thee un-willingly, he has also gone willingly. How many friends hast thou not carried to merry-meetings! How many young parties to the play! How many children, whose faces thou hast turned in an instant from the extremity of lachrymose weariness to that of staring delight. Thou hast contained as many different passions in thee as a human heart; and for the sake of the human heart, old body, thou art venerable. Thou shalt be as respectable as a reduced old gentleman, whose very sloven-liness is pathetic. Thou shalt be made gay, as he is over a younger and richer table, and thou shalt be still more touching for the gaiety.

We wish the hackney-coachman were as interest-ing a machine as either his coach or horses; but it must be owned, that of all the driving species he is the least agreeable specimen. This is partly to be attributed to the life which has most probably put him into his situation; partly to his want of out-side passengers to cultivate his gentility; and partly to the disputable nature of his fare, which always leads him to be lying and cheating. The water-man of the stand, who beats him if possible in sor-didness of appearance, is more respectable. He is less of a vagabond, and cannot cheat you. Nor is the hackney-coachman only disagreeable in himself, but, like Falstaff reversed, the cause of disagreeableness in others; for he sets people upon disputing with him in pettiness and ill-temper. He induces the mercenary to be violent, and the violent to seem mercenary. A man whom you took for a pleasant laughing fellow, shall all of a sudden put on an irritable look of calculation, and vow that he will be charged with a constable, rather than pay the sixpence. Even fair woman shall waive her all-conquering softness, and sound a shrill trumpet in reprobation of the extortionate charioteer, whom, if she were a man, she says, she would expose. Being a woman, then, let her not expose herself. Oh, but it is intolerable to be so imposed upon! Let the lady, then, get a pocketbook, if she must, with the hackney-coach fares in it; or a pain in the legs, rather than the temper; or, above all, let her get wiser, and have an understanding that can dispense with the good opinion of the hackney-coachman. Does she think that her rosy lips were made to grow pale about two-and-sixpence; or that the expression of them will ever be like her cousin Fanny's, if she goes on?

The stage-coachman likes the boys on the road, because he knows they admire him.[1] The hackney-coachman knows that they cannot admire him, and that they can get up behind his coach, which makes him very savage. The cry of "Cut behind!" from the malicious urchins on the pavement, wounds at once his self-love and his interest. He would not mind overloading his master's horses for another sixpence, but to do it for nothing is

[1] Cf. p. 92, "He knows that the boys admire him."—ED.

what shocks his humanity. He hates the boy for imposing upon him, and the boys for reminding him that he has been imposed upon; and he would willingly twinge the cheeks of all nine. The cut of his whip over the coach is very malignant. He has a constant eye to the road behind him. He has also an eye to what may be left in the coach. He will undertake to search the straw for you, and miss the half-crown on purpose. He speculates on what he may get above his fare, according to your manners or company; and knows how much to ask for driving faster or slower than usual. He does not like wet weather so much as people suppose; for he says it rots both his horses and harness, and he takes parties out of town when the weather is fine, which produces good payments in a lump. Lovers, late supper-eaters, and girls going home from boarding-school, are his best pay. He has a rascally air of remonstrance when you dispute half the over-charge, and according to the temper he is in, begs you to consider his bread, hopes you will not make such a fuss about a trifle; or tells you, you may take his number or sit in the coach all night.

*Lady.* There, Sir!

*Indicator* (looking all about him). Where, Ma'am?

*Lady.* The coachman, Sir!

*Indicator.* Oh pray, Madam, don't trouble yourself. Leave the gentleman alone with him. Do you continue to be delightful at a little distance.

A great number of ludicrous adventures must have taken place, in which hackney-coaches were concerned. The story of the celebrated harlequin Lunn, who secretly pitched himself out of one into a tavern window, and when the coachman was about to submit to the loss of his fare, astonished him by calling out again from the inside, is too well known for repetition. There is one of Swift, not perhaps so common. He was going, one dark evening, to dine with some great man, and was accompanied by some other clergymen, to whom he gave their cue. They were all in their canonicals. When they arrive at the house, the coachman opens the door, and lets down the steps. Down steps the Dean, very reverendly in his black robes ; after him comes another personage, equally black and dignified ; then another ; then a fourth. The coachman, who recollects taking up no greater number, is about to put up the steps, when another clergyman descends. After giving way to this other, he proceeds with great confidence to toss them up, when lo ! another comes. Well, there cannot, he thinks, be well more than six. He is mistaken. Down comes a seventh, then an eighth ; then a ninth ; all with decent intervals ; the coach, in the mean time, rocking as if it were giving birth to so many dæmons. The coachman can conclude no less. He cries out, " The devil ! the devil ! " and is preparing to run away, when they all burst into laughter at the success of their joke. They had gone round as they descended, and got in at the other door.

We remember in our boyhood an edifying comment on the proverb of "all is not gold that glistens." The spectacle made such an impression upon us, that we recollect the very spot, which was at the corner of a road in the way from West-minster to Kennington, near a stonemason's. It was a severe winter, and we were out on a holiday, thinking, perhaps, of the gallant hardships to which the ancient soldiers accustomed themselves, when we suddenly beheld a group of hackney-coachmen, not, as Spenser says of his witch,

> Busy, as *seemed*, about some wicked gin,

but pledging each other in what appeared to us to be little glasses of cold water. What temperance, thought we! What extraordinary and noble con-tent! What more than Roman simplicity! There are a set of poor Englishmen, of the homeliest order, in the very depth of winter, quenching their patient and honourable thirst with modicums of cold water! O true virtue and courage! O sight worthy of the Timoleons and Epaminondases! We know not how long we remained in this error; but the first time we recognized the white devil for what it was—the first time we saw through the chrystal purity of its appearance—was a great blow to us. We did not then know what the drinkers went through; and this reminds us that we have omitted one great redemption of the hackney-coachman's character—his being at the mercy of all sorts of chances and weathers. Other drivers have their settled hours and pay. He only is at the mercy of every call and every casualty; he only is dragged without notice, like the damned in Milton, into the extremities of wet and cold, from his alehouse fire to the freezing rain; he only must go any where, at what hour and to whatever place you choose, his old rheumatic limbs shaking under his weight of rags, and the snow and sleet beating into his puckered face, through streets which the wind scours like a channel.[1]

# [FROM] A VISIT TO THE ZOOLO-GICAL GARDENS.

["New Monthly Magazine," Aug. 1836. "Men, Women, and Books," 1847.   C. Kent, 1889.]

 WENT to the Zoological Gardens the other day, for the first time, to see my old friends, "the wild beasts" (grim intimates of boyhood), and enjoy their lift in the world from their lodgings in Towers and Exeter Changes, where they had no air, and where I remember an elephant wearing boots, because the rats gnawed his feet!   The first thing that struck me, next to the beauty of the Gardens, and the pleasant thought that such flowery places were now prepared for creatures whom we lately thrust into mere dens and dust-holes, was the quantity of life and energy presented to one's eyes! What   motion!—What   strength!—What   active elegance!   What prodigious chattering, and brilliant colours in the macaws and parrakeets! What fresh, clean, and youthful salience in the *lynx!* What a variety of dogs, all honest fellows apparently, of the true dog kind; and how bounding,

[1] One of C. Lamb's favourite papers.   See "Autobiography," p. 250.

how intelligent, how fit to guard our doors and
our children, and scamper all over the country
And then the *Persian* greyhound ! How like a
*patrician* dog (better even than Landseer's), and
made as if expressly to wait upon a Persian prince :
its graceful slenderness, darkness, and long silken
ears, matching his own gentlemanly figure and
well-dressed beard !

### THE BEAR.

It is curious to find oneself (literally) hand and
glove with a bear ; giving him buns, and watching
his face, like a schoolboy's, to see how he likes
them. A reflection rises—"if it were not for
those bars, perhaps he would be eating *me*." Yet
how mild they and his food render him. We
scrutinize his countenance and manners at leisure,
and are amused with his apparently indolent yet
active lumpishness, his heavy kind of intelligence
which will do nothing more than is necessary, his
almost hand-like use of his long, awkward-looking
toes, and the fur which he wears clumsily about
him like a' watchman's great-coat. The darker
bears look somehow more natural ; at least to
those whose imaginations have not grown up
amidst polar narrative. The white bear in these
Gardens has a horrible mixed look of innocence
and cruelty. Some Roman tyrant kept a bear as
one of his executioners, and called it "Innocence."
We could imagine it to have had just such a face.
From that smooth, unimpressible aspect there is
no appeal. He has no ill-will to you ; only he is
fond of your flesh, and would eat you up as meekly

as you would sup milk, or swallow a custard.
Imagine his arms around you, and your fate depending upon what you could say to him. You feel
that you might as well talk to a devouring statue,
or to the sign of the " Bear" in Piccadilly, or to a
guillotine, or to the cloak of Nessus, or to your
own great-coat (to ask it to be not so heavy), or to
the smooth-faced wife of an ogre, hungry and deaf,
and one that did not understand your language. [1]

### THE ELEPHANT.

The more one considers an elephant, the more
he makes good his claim to be considered the
Doctor Johnson of the brute creation. He is huge,
potent, sapient, susceptible of tender impressions ;
is a good fellow : likes as much water as the other
did tea ; gets on at a great uncouth rate when he
walks ; and though perhaps less irritable and
melancholy, can take a witty revenge ; as witness
the famous story of the tailor that pricked him, and
whom he drenched with ditch-water. If he were
suddenly gifted with speech, and we asked him
whether he liked his imprisonment, the first words
he would utter would unquestionably be—" Why,
no, sir." Nor is it to be doubted, when going to
dinner, that he would echo the bland sentiment of
our illustrious metropolitan, on a like occasion,
" Sir, I like to dine." If asked his opinion of his
keeper, he would say, " Why, sir, Hipkins is,

[1] " [This] animal resembles many respectable gentlemen
whom we could name. When he wishes to attack anybody
he rises on his hind legs, as men do in the House of Com-
mons."—*Table Talk*, 1851.

upon the whole, 'a good fellow'—like myself (*smiling*)—but not quite so considerate ; he knows I love him, and presumes a little too much upon my forbearance. He teases me for the amusement of the bystanders. Sir, Hipkins takes the display of allowance for the merit of ascendancy."

This is what the elephant manifestly thought on the present occasion ; for the keeper set a little dog at him, less to the amusement of the bystanders than he fancied ; and the noble beast, after butting the cur out of the way, and taking care to spare him as he advanced (for one tread of his foot would have smashed the little pertinacious wretch as flat as a pancake), suddenly made a stop, and, in rebuke of both of them, uttered a high indignant scream, much resembling a score of cracked trumpets.

# A LETTER TO THE BELLS OF A PARISH CHURCH IN ITALY.[1]

### ["New Monthly Magazine," 1825.]

FOR God's sake, dear bells, why this eternal noise? Why do you make this everlasting jangling and outcry? Is it not enough that the whole village talk, but you must be talking too? Are you the representative of all the gossip in the neighbourhood? Now, they tell me, you inform us that a friar is

[1] In this article use has been made of a copy in the possession of Mr. Alexander Ireland, containing corrections in the handwriting of Leigh Hunt.—ED.

dead : now you jingle a blessing on the vines and
olives, "babbling o' green fields : " anon you start
away in honour of a marriage, and jangle as if the
devil were in you.   Your zeal for giving information
may be generous where there are no newspapers ;
but when you have once informed us that a friar is
dead, where is the necessity of repeating the same
intelligence for twelve hours together ?   Did any
one ever hear of a newspaper which contained
nothing from beginning to end but a series of paragraphs, informing us that a certain gentleman was
no more ?

> Died yesterday, Father Paul—
> Died yesterday, Father Paul—
> Died yesterday, Father Paul—

and so on from nine in the morning till nine at
night ? You shall have some information in return,
very necessary to be known by all the bells in
Christendom.   Learn then, sacred, but at the same
time thoughtless tintinnabularies, that there are
dying, as well as dead, people in the world, and
sick people who will die if they are not encouraged.
What must be the effect of this mortal note un-
ceasingly reiterated in their ears ?   Who would set
a whining fellow at a sick man's door to repeat to
him all day long, "Your neighbour's dead ;—your
neighbour's dead."

But you say, " It is to remind the healthy, and
not the dying, that we sound ; and the few must
give way to the many."   Good : it delights me to
hear you say so, because everything will of course
be changed in the economy of certain governments,

except yourselves. But in this particular instance allow me to think you are mistaken. I differ from a belfry with hesitation. Triple bob majors are things before which it becomes a philosophic inquirer to be modest. But have we not memorandums enough to this good end? Have we not coughs, colds, fevers, plethoras, deaths of all sorts occurring round about us, old faces, churchyards, accidents infinite, books, cookery books, wars, apothecaries, gin-shops? You remind the sick and the dying too forcibly: but you are much mistaken if you think that others regard your importunity of advice in any other light than that of a nuisance. They may get used to it; but what then? So much the worse for your admonitions. In like manner they get used to a hundred things which do them no sort of good; which only tend to keep their moods and tempers in a duller state of exasperation.

Then the marriages. Dear bells, do you ever consider that there are people who have been married two years, as well as two hours. What here becomes of your maxim of the few giving way to the many? Have all the rest of the married people, think you, made each other deaf, so that they cannot hear the sound? It may be sport to the new couple, but it is death to the old ones. If a pair or so love one another almost as much as if they had never been married, at least they are none the better for you. If they look kindly at one another when they hear the sound, do you think it is not in spite of the bells, as well as for sweetness of recollection?

I.            I

In my country it is bad enough.   A bell shall go
for hours telling us that Mr. Ching is dead.

"Ring, ring, ring—Ching, Ching, Ching—Oh
Ching!—Ah Ching, Ching! I say—Ching is gone
—Gone, gone, gone—Good people, listen to the
steeple—Ching, Ching, Ching."

"Ay," says a patient in his bed, "*I* knew him.
He had the same palsy as I have."

"Mercy on us," cries an old woman in the next
house, "there goes poor Mr. Ching, sure enough."

"I just had a pleasant thought," says a sick
mourner, "and now that bell! that melancholy
bell!"

"The bell will go for me, mother, soon," observes a poor child to its weeping parent.

"What will become of my poor children?" exclaims a dying father.

It would be useful to know how many deaths are
hastened by a bell : at least how many recoveries
are retarded.   There are sensitive persons, not
otherwise in ill-health, who find it difficult to hear
the sound without tears.   What must they feel on
a sick bed!   As for the unfeeling, who are the
only persons to be benefited, they care for it no
more than for the postman's.

But in England we can at least reckon upon
shorter bell-ringings, and upon long intervals without any.   We have not bells every day as they
have here, except at the universities.   The saints
in the protestant calendar are quiet.   Our belfries
also are thicker ; the clappers do not come swinging and flaring out of window, like so many scolds.
Italians talk of music ; but I must roundly ask,

how came Italian ears to put up with this music of the Chinese? But you belong to that corner of earth exclusively, and ought all to return thither. I am loth to praise anything Mussulman in these times ; but to give the Turk his due, he is not addicted to superfluous noise. His belfry-men cannot deafen a neighbourhood all day long with the death of an Imaun, for they are themselves the bells. Alas ! why do not steeples catch cold, and clappers require a gargle? Why must things that have no feeling—belfries, and one's advisers—be exclusively gifted with indefatigability of tongue?

Lastly, your tunes ! I thought, in Italy, that anything which undertook to be musical, would be in some way or other truly so—harmonious, if not various ; various and new, if not very harmonious. But I must say our bells in England have double your science. I once sang a duet with St. Clement's Church in the Strand. Indeed, I have often done it, returning from a symposium in the Temple. The tune was the hundred and fourth psalm. I took the second. And this reminds me that our English bells have the humanity to catch a cold now and then, or something like it. They will lose two or three of their notes at a time. I used to humour this infirmity in my friend St. Clement's, as became an old acquaintance, and always waited politely till he resumed. But in Italy the bells have the oddest, and at the same time the most unfading and inexorable hops of tunes, that can be imagined.

> Light quirks of music, broken and uneven,
> Make the soul dance upon a jig to heaven.

One might suppose that the steeple, in some un-
accountable fit of merriment, struck up a country-
dance, like that recorded in Mr. Monk Lewis's
account of Orpheus :—

> While an arm of the sea,
> Introduced by a tree,
> To a fair young whale advances ;
> And making a leg,
> Says, " Miss, may I beg
> Your fin for the two next dances?"

I used to wonder at this, till one day I heard
the host announced in a procession by as merry a
set of fiddles, as ever played to a ship's company.
The other day a dead bishop was played out in
church to the tune of *Di piacer*. But I forget I
am writing a letter ; and luckily my humour, as
well as my paper, is out. Besides, the bells have
left off before me ; for which I am their

Much obliged, exhausted humble servant,
MISOCROTALUS.

## THE TRUE ENJOYMENT OF SPLEN-
## DOUR—A CHINESE APOLOGUE.

["The Reflector," No. III., Art. XIX., 1812. "A Day
by the Fire," 1870.]

DOUBTLESS, saith the illustrious Me,
he that gaineth much possession hath
need of the wrists of Hong and the
seriousness of Shan-Fee, since palaces
are not built with a teaspoon, nor are to be kept

by one who runneth after butterflies. But above all it is necessary that he who carrieth a great burden, whether of gold or silver, should hold his head as lowly as is necessary, lest in lifting it on high he bring his treasure to nought, and lose with the spectators the glory of true gravity, which is meekness.

Quo, who was the son of Quee, who was the son of Quee-Fong, who was the five hundred and fiftieth in lineal descent from the ever-to-be-remembered Fing, chief minister of the Emperor Yau, one day walked out into the streets of Pekin in all the lustre of his rank. Quo, besides the greatness of his birth and the multitude of his accomplishments, was a courtier of the first order, and his pigtail was proportionate to his merits, for it hung down to the ground and kissed the dust as it went with its bunch of artificial roses. Ten huge and sparkling rings, which encrusted his hands with diamonds, and almost rivalled the sun that struck on them, led the ravished eyes of the beholders to the more precious enormity of his nails, which were each an inch long, and by proper nibbing might have taught the barbarians of the West to look with just scorn on their many writing-machines. But even these were nothing to the precious stones that covered him from head to foot. His bonnet, in which a peacock's feather was stuck in a most engaging manner, was surmounted by a sapphire of at least the size of a pigeon's egg; his shoulders and sides sustained a real burden of treasure; and as he was one of the handsomest men at court, being exceedingly corpulent, and, indeed, as his flatterers gave out, hardly able to walk, it may be imagined that he proceeded at no undignified pace. He would have ridden in his sedan had he been lighter of body; but so much unaffected corpulence was not to be concealed, and he went on foot that nobody might suspect him of pretending to a dignity he did not possess. Behind him, three servants attended, clad in most gorgeous silks; the middle one held his umbrella over his head; he on the right bore a fan of ivory, whereon were carved the exploits of Whay-Quang; and he on the left sustained a purple bag on each arm, one containing opium and Areca-nut, the other the ravishing preparation of Gin-Seng, which possesses the Five Relishes. All the servants looked the same way as their master—that is to say, straightforward, with their eyes majestically half-shut, only they cried every now and then with a loud voice, "Vanish before the illustrious Quo, favourite of the mighty Brother of the Sun and Moon."

Though the favourite looked neither to the right nor to the left, he could not but perceive the great homage that was paid him as well by the faces as the voices of the multitude. But one person, a Bonze, seemed transported beyond all the rest with an enthusiasm of admiration, and followed at a respectful distance from his side, bowing to the earth at every ten paces, and exclaiming, "Thanks to my lord for his jewels!" After repeating this for about six times, he increased the expressions of his gratitude, and said, "Thanks to my illustrious lord from his poor servant for his glorious jewels,"

—and then again, " Thanks to my illustrious lord, whose eye knoweth not degradation, from his poor servant, who is not fit to exist before him, for his jewels that make the rays of the sun like ink." In short, the man's gratitude was so great, and its language delivered in phrases so choice, that Quo could contain his curiosity no longer, and turning aside, demanded to know his meaning. " I have not given you the jewels," said the favourite, "and why should you thank me for them ?"

" Refulgent Quo !" answered the Bonze, again bowing to the earth, " what you say is as true as the five maxims of Fo, who was born without a father ; but your slave repeats his thanks, and is indeed infinitely obliged. You must know, O dazzling son of Quee, that of all my sect I have perhaps the greatest taste for enjoying myself. Seeing my lord therefore go by, I could not but be transported at having so great a pleasure, and said to myself, ' The great Quo is very kind to me and my fellow-citizens : he has taken infinite labour to acquire his magnificence, he takes still greater pains to preserve it, and all the while, I, who am lying under a shed, enjoy it for nothing.' "

A hundred years after, when the Emperor Whang heard this story, he diminished the expenditure of his household one half, and ordered the dead Bonze to be raised to the rank of a Colao.[1]

[1] " How the Chinese came to invent tea, as Sancho would say, we do not know ; but it is the most ingenious, humane, and poetical of their discoveries. It is their epic poem " ("The Indicator,—Table Wits at Breakfast ").

# WIT MADE EASY

## OR A HINT TO WORD-CATCHERS.[1]

["New Monthly Magazine," May, 1825. "Printing Machine," July, 1835. "Wishing Cap Papers," 1874.]

### A.

HERE comes B., the liveliest yet most tiresome of word-catchers. I wonder whether he'll have wit enough to hear good news óf his mistress.—Well, B., my dear boy, I hope I see you well.

*B.* I hope you do, my dear A., otherwise you have lost your eyesight.

*A.* Good. Well, how do you do?

*B.* How? Why as other people do. You would not have me eccentric, would you?

*A.* Nonsense. I mean, how do you find yourself?

*B.* Find myself! Where's the necessity of finding myself? I have not been lost.

*A.* Incorrigible dog! come now; to be serious.

*B.* (*comes closer to A. and looks very serious*).

*A.* Well, what now?

*B.* I am come, to be serious.

*A.* Come now; nonsense, B., leave off this. (*Laying his hand on his arm.*)

*B.* (*looking down at his arm*). I can't leave off

---

[1] In this article use has been made of a copy in the possession of Mr. Alexander Ireland, containing corrections in the handwriting of Leigh Hunt.—ED.

this.   It would look very absurd to go without a sleeve.

*A.* Ah, ha!  You make me laugh in spite of myself.   How's Jackson?

*B.* The deuce he is!  How's Jackson, is he? Well I never should have thought that.   How can Howe be Jackson?  "Surname and arms," I suppose, of some rich uncle?  I have not seen him gazetted.

*A.* Good-bye.

*B.* (*detaining him*).  "Good Bye!"  What a sudden enthusiasm in favour of some virtuous man of the name of Bye!  "*Good* Bye!"—To think of Ashton standing at the corner of the street, doating aloud on the integrity of a Mr. Bye!

*A.* Ludicrous enough.  I can't help laughing, I confess.  But laughing does not always imply merriment.  You do not delight us, Jack, with these sort of jokes, but tickle us; and tickling may give pain.

*B.* Don't accept it then.  You need not take everything that is given you.

*A.* You'll want a straightforward answer some day, and then——

*B.* You'll describe a circle about me, before you give it.  Well, that's your affair, not mine.  You'll astonish the natives, that's all.

*A.* It's great nonsense, you must allow.

*B.* I can't see why *it* is greater nonsense than any other pronoun.

*A.* (*in despair*).  Well, it's of no use, I see.

*B.* Excuse me: *it* is of the very greatest use.  I don't know a part of speech more useful.  *It* per-

forms all the greatest offices of nature, and contains, in fact, the whole agency and mystery of the
world.   *It* rains.   *It* is fine weather.   *It* freezes.
*It* thaws.   *It* (which is very odd) is one o'clock.
" *It* has been a very frequent observation."   *It*
goes.   Here it goes.   How goes it ?—(which, by
the way, is a translation from the Latin, *Eo, is, it* ;
*Eo,* I go ; *is,* thou goest ; *it,* he or it goes.   In
short——

*A.* In short, if I wanted a dissertation on *it,*
now's the time for it.   But I don't ; so, good bye.
(*Going*)—I saw Miss M. last night.

*B.* The devil you did !   Where was it ?

*A.* (*to himself*).   Now I have him, and will
revenge myself.   Where *was* it ?   Where was *it,*
eh ?  Oh, you must know a great deal more about
*it* than I do.

*B.* Nay, my dear fellow, do tell me.   I'm on
thorns.

*A.* On thorns !   Very odd thorns.   I never saw
an acanthus look so like a pavement.

*B.* Come now, to be serious.

*A.* (*comes close to B. and looks tragic*).

*B.* He, he !   Very fair, egad.   But do tell me
now where was she ?   How did she look ?   Who
was with her ?

*A.* Oh, ho !  *Hoo* was with her, was he ?   Well,
I wanted to know his name.   I couldn't tell
who the devil it was.   But I say, Jack, *who's*
Hoo ?

*B.* Good.   He, he !   Devilish fair !   But now,
my dear Will, for God's sake, you know how
interested I am.

*A.* The deuce you are ! I always took you for a disinterested fellow. I always said of Jack B., Jack's apt to overdo his credit for wit ; but a more honest disinterested fellow I never met with.

*B.* Well, then, as you think so, be merciful. Where is Miss M. ?

*A.* This is more astonishing news than any. *Ware* is Miss M. I know her passion for music ; but this is wonderful. Good Heavens ! To think of a delicate young lady dressing herself in man's clothes, and leading the band at a theatre under the name of Ware.

*B.* Now, my dear Will, consider. I acknowledge I have been tiresome ; I confess it is a bad habit, this word-catching ; but consider my love.

*A.* (*falls in an attitude of musing*).

*B.* Well.

*A.* Don't interrupt me. I am considering your love.

*B.* I repent ; I am truly sorry. What shall I do ? (*laying his hand on his heart*).—I'll give up this cursed habit.

*A.* You will ?—upon honour ?

*B.* Upon my honour.

*A.* On the spot ?

*B.* Now, this instant. Now, and for ever.

*A.* Strip away, then.

*B.* Strip ? for what?

*A.* You said you'd give up that cursed habit.

*B.* Now, my dear A., for the love of everything that is sacred ; for the love of your *own* love——

*A.* Will you promise me sincerely ?

*B.* Heart and soul.

*A.* Step over the way, then, into the coffee-house, and I'll tell you.

*Street-sweeper.* Plase your honour, pray remember the poor swape.

*B.* My friend, I'll never forget you, if that will be of any service. I'll think of you next year.

*A.* What again !

*B.* The last time, as I hope to be saved. Here, my friend; there's a shilling for you. Charity covers a multitude of bad jokes.

*Street-sweeper.* God send your honour thousands of them.

*B.* The jokes or the shillings, you rascal?

*Street-sweeper.* Och, the shillings. Divil a bit the bad jokes. I can make them myself, and a shilling's no joke any how.

*A.* What ! really silent ! and in spite of the dog's equivocal Irish face ! Come, B., I now see you can give up a jest, and are really in love ; and your mistress, I will undertake to say, will not be sorry to be convinced of both. Women like to begin with merriment well enough ; but they prefer coming to a grave conclusion.

# THE PRINCE ON ST. PATRICK'S DAY.

["Examiner," March 22nd, 1812.  "Autobiography,"
1850.]

THE same page [of "The Morning Post"]
contained also a set of wretched commonplace lines in French, Italian,
Spanish, and English, *literally* address-
ing the Prince Regent in the following terms,
among others :—"You are the *Glory of the people*"
—"You are the *Protector of the Arts*"—"You are
the *Mæcenas of the age*"—"Wherever you appear
*you conquer all hearts*, wipe away tears, excite
*desire and love*, and win *beauty* towards you"—
"You breathe *eloquence*"—"You inspire the
Graces"—"You are *Adonis in loveliness.*"  "Thus
gifted" it proceeds in English,—

> Thus gifted with each grace of mind,
> Born to delight and bless mankind ;
> Wisdom, with Pleasure in her train,
> Great Prince ! shall signalize thy reign :
> To Honour, Virtue, Truth allied ;
> The nation's safeguard and its pride ;
> With monarchs of immortal fame
> Shall bright renown enrol the name.

What person, unacquainted with the true state of
the case, would imagine, in reading these astounding eulogies, that this "*Glory of the people*" was
the subject of millions of shrugs and reproaches !
—that this "*Protector of the Arts*" had named a
wretched foreigner for his historical painter, in

disparagement or in ignorance of the merits of his own countrymen !—that this "*Mæcenas of the age*" patronized not a single deserving writer ! that this " *Breather of eloquence* " could not say a few decent extempore words—if we are to judge, at least, from what he said to his regiment on its embarkation for Portugal !—that this "*Conqueror of hearts* " was the disappointer of hopes !—that this " *Exciter of desire* " [bravo ! Messieurs of the " Post ! "]—this "*Adonis in loveliness* " was a corpulent man of fifty !—in short, that this *delightful, blissful, wise, pleasurable, honourable, virtuous, true,* and *immortal* prince, was a violator of his word, a libertine over head and ears in disgrace, a despiser of domestic ties, the companion of gamblers and demireps, a man who has just closed half a century without one single claim on the gratitude of his country, or the respect of posterity ! [1]

---

[1] " This article, no doubt, was very bitter and contemptuous ; therefore in the legal sense of the term very libellous ; the more so, inasmuch as it was very true . . . . it did but express what all the world were feeling."—" Autobiography of L. H.," 1850.

The above is the most stinging portion of the article for which Leigh Hunt and his brother John (the proprietor and publisher of " The Examiner ") were imprisoned from Feb. 1813 to Feb. 1815. Lord Brougham's eloquent defence of the libel is a masterpiece of ingenious irony. See " Bibliography," No. 62.—ED.

The Chapel.
Horsemonger Lane
Jail.

# AN ANSWER TO THE QUESTION, WHAT IS POETRY?

### ["Imagination and Fancy," 1844.]

POETRY, strictly and artistically so called, that is to say, considered not merely as poetic feeling, which is more or less shared by all the world, but as the operation of that feeling, such as we see it in the poet's book, is the utterance of a passion for truth, beauty, and power, embodying and illustrating its conceptions by imagination and fancy, and modulating its language on the principle of variety in uniformity. Its means are whatever the universe contains ; and its ends, pleasure and exaltation. Poetry stands between nature and convention, keeping alive among us the enjoyment of the external and the spiritual world : it has constituted the most enduring fame of nations; and, next to Love and Beauty, which are its parents, is the greatest proof to man of the pleasure to be found in all things, and of the probable riches of infinitude. . . .

Poetry is imaginative passion. The quickest and subtlest test of the possession of its essence is in expression ; the variety of things to be expressed shows the amount of its resources ; and the continuity of the song completes the evidence of its strength and greatness. He who has thought, feeling, expression, imagination, action, character, and continuity, all in the largest amount and highest degree, is the greatest poet. . . .

and hubbubs of Animal Spirits ;—all so general
yet particular, so demanding distinct recognition,
and yet so baffling the attempt with their numbers
and their confusion, that a thousand masquerades
in one would have seemed to threaten less torment
to the pen of a reporter.

    \*       \*       \*       \*       \*

[It is not to be supposed] that everything witty or
humorous excites laughter.  It may be accompanied with a sense of too many other things to do
so ; with too much thought, with too great a perfection even, or with pathos and sorrow.  All extremes meet; excess of laughter itself runs into tears,
and mirth becomes heaviness.  Mirth itself is too
often but melancholy in disguise.  The jests of the
fool in " Lear " are the sighs of knowledge.  But
as far as Wit and Humour affect us on their own
accounts, or unmodified by graver considerations,
laughter is their usual result and happy ratification. . . .

Wit is the clash and reconcilement of incongruities ; the meeting of extremes round a corner; the
flashing of an artificial light from one object to
another, disclosing some unexpected resemblance
or connection.  It is the detection of likeness in
unlikeness, of sympathy in antipathy, or of the
extreme points of antipathies themselves, made
friends by the very merriment of their introduction.  The mode, or form, is comparatively of no
consequence, provided it give no trouble to the
apprehension : and you may bring as many ideas
together as can pleasantly assemble.  But a single
one is nothing.  Two-ideas are as necessary to

Wit,[1] as couples are to marriages ; and the union is happy in proportion to the agreeableness of the offspring. . . .

*Humour*, considered as the object treated of by the humorous writer, and not as the power of treating it, derives its name from the prevailing quality of *moisture* in the bodily temperament; and is *a tendency of the mind to run in particular directions of thought or feeling more amusing than accountable ;* at least in the opinion of society. It is, therefore, either in reality or appearance, a thing inconsistent. It deals in incongruities of character and circumstance, as Wit does in those of arbitrary ideas. The more the incongruities the better, provided they are all in nature ; but two, at any rate, are as necessary to Humour, as the two ideas are to Wit ; and the more strikingly they differ yet harmonize, the more amusing the result. Such is the melting together of the propensities to love and war in the person of exquisite Uncle Toby ; of the gullible and the manly in Parson Adams ; of the professional and the individual, or the accidental and the permanent, in the Canterbury Pilgrims ; of the objectionable and the agreeable, the fat and the sharp-witted, in Falstaff ; of honesty and knavery in Gil Blas ; of pretension and non-performance in the Bullies of the dramatic poets ; of folly and wisdom in Don Quixote ; of shrewdness and doltishness in Sancho

---

[1] "That active combination of ideas, called wit, which like the needle finds sympathy in the most remote objects, and almost unites logic with fancy."—Essay on Mackenzie. "Classic Tales."

Panza; and, it may be added, in the discordant yet harmonious co-operation of Don Quixote and his attendant, considered as a pair. . . .

# THE REPRESENTATION OF TRAGEDY.

[" The News," 1805. " Critical Essays on the Performances of the London Theatres," 1807.]

THE drama is the most perfect imitation of human life; by means of the stage it represents man in all his varieties of mind, his expressions of manner, and his power of action, and is the first of moralities because it teaches us in the most impressive way the knowledge of ourselves When its lighter species, which professes to satirize, forsakes this imitation for caricature it becomes farce, whether it still be denominated *comedy*, as we say the *comedies* of REYNOLDS, or whether it be called *opera*, as we say the *operas* of CHERRY and COBB : the actors in these pieces must act unnaturally or they will do nothing, but in real comedy they will act naturally for the same reason. In the graver kind of drama, however, their imitation of life is perfect ; not as it copies real and simple manners, but as it accords with our habitual ideas of human character ; those who have produced the general idea that tragedy and comedy are equally direct imitations of human life, have mistaken their habitual for their experimental knowledge. The loftier persons of tragedy require an elevation of language and manner, which

they never use in real life. Heroes and sages speak
like other men, they use their action as carelessly
and their looks as indifferently, and are not distinguished from their fellow-mortals by their personal but by their mental character; but the popular
conception of a great man delights in dignifying
his external habits, not only because great men are
rarely seen, and therefore acquire dignity by con-
cealment, but because we conclude that they who
excel us so highly in important points can have
nothing unimportant about them. We can hardly
persuade ourselves, for instance, that SHAKESPEARE
ever disputed in a club, or that MILTON was fond of
smoking : the ideas of greatness and insignificance
associate with difficulty, and as extreme associations
are seldom formed but by minds of peculiar fancy
and vigorous thought, it is evident they will be
rarely entertained by the majority of the world.
A tragic hero, who called for his follower or his
horse, would in real life call for him as easily and
carelessly as any other man, but in tragedy such a
carelessness would become ludicrous : the loftiness
of his character must be universal ; an artist who
would paint the battles of Frederic of Prussia in a
series of pictures would study to maintain this important character throughout, he would not represent the chief sitting on horseback in a slovenly
manner and taking snuff, though the snuff-box
no doubt was of much importance in those days to
his majesty, who as POPE says of PRINCE EUGENE,
was as great a taker of snuff as of towns : so great
a violence of contrast would become caricature in
painting, and in tragedy it would degenerate into

burlesque. Tragedy is an imitation of life in passions; it is comedy only which imitates both passions and habits.

A tragic actor then is to be estimated, not as he always copies nature, but as he satisfies the general opinion of life and manners. He must neither on the one hand debase his dignity by too natural a simplicity of manner, nor on the other give it a ridiculous elevation by pompousness and bombast. He cannot draw much of his knowledge from real life, because the loftier passions are rarely exhibited in the common intercourse of mankind; but nevertheless he should not indulge himself in novelties of invention, because the hearts of his audience will be able to judge where their experience has no power. Much study should strengthen his judgment, since he must perfectly understand before he can feel his author and teach others to feel; where there is strong natural genius, judgment will usually follow in the development of great passions, but it may fail in the minute proprieties of the stage: where there is not a strong natural genius, the contrary will be generally found. For the common actions of great characters he must study the manner of the stage, for their passions nothing but nature.

## TABLE TALK.

["The Atlas," March 14th, 1846. "Table Talk," 1851.
C. Kent, 1889.]

TABLE-TALK, to be perfect, should be sincere without bigotry, differing without discord, sometimes grave, always agreeable, touching on deep points, dwelling most on seasonable ones, and letting everybody speak and be heard. During the wine after dinner, if the door of the room be opened, there sometimes comes bursting up the drawing-room stairs a noise like that of a tap-room. Everybody is shouting in order to make himself audible ; argument is tempted to confound itself with loudness ; and there is not one conversation going forward, but six, or a score. This is better than formality and want of spirits ; but it is no more the right thing, than a scramble is a dance, or the tap-room chorus a quartette of Rossini. The perfection of conversational intercourse is when the breeding of high life is animated by the fervour of genius.

# SPENSER.[1]

## [BORN 1552—DIED 1598.]

[From an article on his poetry in "Tait's Edinburgh Magazine," Sept. 1833, being "The Wishing Cap" (New Series), No. VI.]

DIVINE Poet ! sitting in the midst of thy endless treasures, thy luxurious landscapes, and thy descending gods ! Fantastic as Nature's self in the growth of some few flowers of thy creation ; beauteous and perfect as herself, [in] the rest. We have found consolation in thee at times when almost everything pained us, and when we could find it in no other poet of thy nation, because the world into which they took us was not equally remote. Shakespeare, with all our love and reverence for him, has still kept us among men and their cares, even in his enchanted island and his summer-night dreams. Milton will not let us breathe the air of his Paradise, undistressed by the hauntings of theology, and the shadows of what was to come. Chaucer has left his only romance unfinished, and will not relieve us of his emotion but by mirth, and that not always such as we can be merry with, or as he would have liked himself had he fallen upon times worthier of him. But in coming to thee, we have travelled in one instant thousands of miles,

1 Leigh Hunt imitated Spenser in his youth, and praised him throughout his life, see his works—*passim*, especially the sonnet, "The Poets," in vol. ii.—ED.

and to a quarter in which no sin of reality is heard. Even its warfare is that of poetical children ; of demi-gods playing at romance. Around us are the woods ; in our distant ear is the sea ; the glimmering forms that we behold are those of nymphs and deities ; or a hermit makes the loneliness more lonely ; or we hear a horn blow, and the ground trembling with the coming of a giant ; and our boyhood is again existing, full of belief, though its hair be turning grey ; because thou, a man, hast rewritten its books, and proved the surpassing riches of its wisdom.

# SHAKESPEARE.[1]

## [BORN 1564—DIED 1616.]

### ["Wit and Humour," 1846.  C. Kent, 1889.]

SHAKESPEARE had as great a comic genius as tragic ; and everybody would think so, were it possible for comedy to impress the mind as tragedy does. It is true, the times he lived in, as Hazlitt has remarked, were not so foppish and ridiculous as those of our prose comic dramatists, and therefore he had not so much to laugh at : and it is observed by the same critic, with equal truth, that his genius was of too large and magnanimous a description to delight in satire. But who doubts that had Shakespeare lived in those inferior times, the author of the character of Mercutio could have written that

[1] See also "Imagination and Fancy."—ED.

of Dorimant? of Benedick and Beatrice, the dia·
logues of Congreve? or of " Twelfth Night " and
the " Taming of the Shrew," the most uproarious
farce? I certainly cannot think with Dr. Johnson
that he wrote comedy better than tragedy; that
" his tragedy seems to be skill, and his comedy
instinct." I could as soon believe that the instinct
of Nature was confined to laughter, and that her
tears were shed upon principles of criticism. Such
may have been the Doctor's recipe for writing
tragedy; but " Irene " is not " King Lear."
Laughter and tears are alike born with us, and so
was the power of exciting them with Shakespeare;
because it pleased Nature to make him a complete
human being.

Shakespeare had wit and humour in perfection;
and like every possessor of powers so happy, he
rioted in their enjoyment. Molière was not fonder
of running down a joke : Rabelais could not give
loose to a more " admirable fooling." His mirth
is commensurate with his melancholy ; it is founded
on the same knowledge and feeling, and it furnished
him with a set-off to their oppression. When he
had been too thoughtful with Hamlet, he " took it
out " with Falstaff and Sir Toby. Not that he was
habitually melancholy. He had too healthy a
brain for that, and too great animal spirits ; but
in running the whole circle of thought, he must of
necessity have gone through its darkest as well as
brightest phases ; and the sunshine was welcome
in proportion. Shakespeare is the inventor of the
phrase, " setting the table in a roar ; " of the
memory of Yorick ; of the stomach of Falstaff,

stuffed as full of wit as of sack. He "wakes the
night-owl with a catch;" draws "three souls out
of one weaver;" passes the "equinoctial of Queu-
bus" (some glorious torrid zone, lying beyond three
o'clock in the morning); and reminds the "unco
righteous" for ever, that virtue, false or true, is
not incompatible with the recreations of "cakes
and ale." Shakespeare is said to have died of
getting out of a sick-bed to entertain his friends
Drayton and Ben Jonson, visitors from London.
He might have died a later and a graver death,
but he could not well have had one more genial,
and therefore more poetical. Far was it from dis-
honouring the eulogizer of "good men's feasts;"
the recorder of the noble friends Antonio and
Bassanio; the great thorough-going humanist, who
did equal justice to the gravest and the gayest moments of life.

It is a remarkable proof of the geniality of Shakespeare's jesting, that even its abundance of ideas
does not spoil it; for, in comedy as well as tragedy,
he is the most reflective of writers. I know but of one
that comes near him in this respect; and very near
him (I dare to affirm) he does come, though he has
none of his poetry, properly so called. It is Sterne;
in whose "Tristram Shandy" there is not a word
without meaning—often of the profoundest as well
as kindliest sort. The professed fools of Shakespeare are among the wisest of men. They talk
Æsop and Solomon in every jest. Yet they amuse
as much as they instruct us. The braggart Parolles,
whose name signifies *words*, as though he spoke
nothing else, scarcely utters a sentence that is not

rich with ideas ; yet his weakness and self-com-
mittals hang over them all like a sneaking infec,
tion, and hinder our laughter from becoming respectful.　The scene in which he is taken blind-
fold among his old acquaintances, and so led to
vilify their characters, under the impression that he
is gratifying their enemies, is almost as good as the
screen-scene in the " School for Scandal."

## BEAUMONT AND FLETCHER.

### [BEAUMONT, 1585—1613.　FLETCHER, 1579 —1625.]

#### [" Wit and Humour," 1846.]

SINCE expressing, in the above volume,[1]
the surprise which everybody feels at
the astounding mixture of license and
refinement displayed by these poets (for
the grossness of earlier writers is but a simplicity
compared with it), I have come to the conclusion
that it was an excess of animal spirits, encouraged
by the demand of the times, and the intoxication
of applause.　They were the sons of men of rank ;
they had been thrown upon the town in the hey-
day of their blood, probably with a turn for lavish
expenditure ; they certainly wanted money as they
advanced, and were glad to get it of gross audiences ;
they had been taught to confound loyalty with
servility, which subjected them to the dissolute influence of the court of James the First ; they came

---

1 *i.e.* " Imagination and Fancy."

among the actors and the playwrights, with advantages of position, perhaps of education and accomplishments, superior to them all : their confidence, their wit, their enjoyment was unbounded ; everybody was glad to hear what the gay gentlemen had to say ; and forth they poured it accordingly, without stint or conscience. Beaumont died young ; but Fletcher, who went writing on, appears to have taken a still greater license than his friend. The son of the bishop had probably been tempted to go farther out of bounds than the son of the judge ; for Dr. Fletcher was not such a bishop as Grindall or Jewel. The poet might have been taught hypocrisy by his father ; and, in despising it as he grew up, had gone to another extreme.

The reader of [these plays] will observe the difference between the fierce weight of the satire of Volpone, in which poison and suffocation are brought in to aggravate, and the gayer caricature of Beaumont and Fletcher. It is equally founded on truth—equally wilful and superabundant in the treatment of it, but more light and happy. You feel that the writers enjoyed it with a gayer laugh. The pretended self-deception with which a coward lies to his own thoughts—the necessity for support which induces him to apply to others as cowardly as himself for the warrant of their good opinion, and the fascinations of vanity which impels such men into the exposure which they fancy they have taken the subtlest steps to guard against—are most entertainingly set forth in the interview of Bassus with the two bullies, and the subsequent catastrophe of all three in the hands of Bacurius. The nice balance of distinction and difference in which the bullies pretend to weigh the merits of kicks and beatings, and the impossibility which they affect of a shadow of imputation against their valours, or even of the power to assume it hypothetically, are masterly plays of wit of the first order.[1]

[1] For a more particular account of Leigh Hunt's opinion of these authors, and especially of the "offences against decency" in their plays, see the "Remarks" prefixed to his selections from them "to the exclusion of whatever is morally objectionable," 1855. "[Where], in a word, is all the best passion and poetry of the two friends, such as I hope and believe they would have been glad to see brought together; such as would have reminded them of those happiest evenings which they spent in the same room, not perhaps when they had most wine in their heads, and were loudest, and merriest, and least pleased, but when they were most pleased both with themselves and with all things,—serene, sequestered, feeling their companionship and their poetry sufficient for them, without needing the ratification of it by its fame, or echo; such evenings as those in which they wrote the description of the boy by the fountain's side, or his confession as Euphrasia, or Caratach's surrender to the Romans, or the address to Sleep in 'Valentinian,' or the divine song on 'Melancholy,' which must have made them feel as if they had created a solitude of their own, and heard the whisper of it stealing by their window." —ED.

# BUTLER.

## [BORN 1612—DIED 1680.]

### [" Wit and Humour," 1846.   C. Kent, 1889.]

**B**UTLER is the wittiest of English poets, and at the same time he is one of the most learned, and what is more, one of the wisest.   His " Hudibras," though naturally the most popular of his works from its size, subject, and witty excess, was an accident of birth and party compared with his Miscellaneous Poems ; yet both abound in thoughts as great and deep as the surface is sparkling ; and his genius altogether, having the additional recommendation of verse, might have given him a fame greater than Rabelais, had his animal spirits been equal to the rest of his qualifications for a universalist.   At the same time, though not abounding in poetic sensibility, he was not without it.   He is author of the touching simile,

*True as the dial to the sun,*
*Although it be not shin'd upon.*

The following is as elegant as anything in Lovelace or Waller :—

—What security's too strong
*To guard that gentle heart from wrong,*
That to its friend is glad to pass
*Itself away, and all it has,*
And like an anchorite, gives over
This world, *for the heaven of a lover !*

And *this*, if read with the seriousness and single-

ness of feeling that become it, is, I think, a comparison full of as much grandeur as cordiality,—

> Like Indian widows, *gone to bed*
> *In flaming curtains to the dead.*

You would sooner have looked for it in one of
Marvell's poems, than in " Hudibras."

Butler has little humour. His two heroes,
Hudibras and Ralph, are not so much humourists
as pedants. They are as little like their prototypes, Don Quixote and Sancho, as two dreary
puppets are unlike excesses of humanity. They
are not even consistent with their other prototypes,
the Puritans, or with themselves, for they are dull
fellows unaccountably gifted with the author's wit.
In this respect, and as a narrative, the poem is a
failure. Nobody ever thinks of the story, except
to wonder at its inefficiency; or of Hudibras himself, except as described at his outset. He is nothing but a ludicrous figure. But considered as a
banter issuing from the author's own lips, on the
wrong side of Puritanism, and indeed on all the
pedantic and hypocritical abuses of human reason,
the whole production is a marvellous compound of
wit, learning, and felicitous execution. The wit is
pure and incessant; the learning as quaint and
out-of-the-way as the subject; the very rhymes are
echoing scourges, made of the peremptory and the
incongruous. This is one of the reasons why the
rhymes have been so much admired. They are
laughable, not merely in themselves, but from the
masterly will and violence with which they are
made to correspond to the absurdities they lash.

The most extraordinary license is assumed as a matter of course; the accentuation jerked out of its place with all the indifference and effrontery of a reason "sufficing unto itself." The poem is so peculiar in this respect, the laughing delight of the reader so well founded, and the passages so sure to be accompanied with a full measure of wit and knowledge, that I have retained its best rhymes throughout, and thus brought them together for the first time.

Butler, like the great wit of the opposite party, Marvel, was an honest man, fonder of his books than of worldly success, and superior to party itself in regard to final principles. He wrote a satire on the follies and vices of the court, which is most likely the reason why it is doubted whether he ever got anything by "Hudibras;" and he was so little prejudiced in favour of the scholarship he possessed, that he vindicated the born poet above the poet of books, and would not have Shakespeare tried by a Grecian standard.

# POPE.

## [BORN 1688—DIED 1744.]

["Wit and Humour," 1846.  C. Kent, 1889.]

ESIDES being an admirable wit and satirist, and a man of the most exquisite good sense, Pope was a true poet ; and though in all probability his entire nature could never have made him a great one

I.                                                                L

(since the whole man contributes to form the genius, and the very weakness of his organization was in the way of it), yet in a different age the boy who wrote the beautiful verses—

Blest be the man whose wish and care,

would have turned out, I think, a greater poet than he was.[1] He had more sensibility, thought, and fancy, than was necessary for the purposes of his school; and he led a sequestered life with his. books and his grotto, caring little for the manners he drew, and capable of higher impulses than had been given him by the wits of the time of Charles the Second. It was unlucky for him (if indeed it did not produce a lucky variety for the reading world) that Dryden came immediately before him. Dryden, a robuster nature, was just great enough to mislead Pope; and French ascendancy completed his fate. Perhaps, after all, nothing better than such a honey and such a sting as this exquisite writer developed, could have been got out of his little delicate pungent nature; and we have every reason to be grateful for what they have done for us. Hundreds of greater pretensions in poetry have not attained to half his fame, nor did they deserve it; for they did not take half his pains. Perhaps they were unable to take them, for want of as good a balance of qualities. Success is generally commensurate with its grounds.

Pope, though a genius of a less masculine order

[1] "What numbers of men, of similar constitutions with Pope, have died of surfeits, and done nothing!"—"Wishing Cap Papers," 1874.

than Dryden, and not possessed of his numbers or his impulsiveness, had more delicacy and fancy, has left more passages that have become proverbial, and was less confined to the region of matter of fact. Dryden never soared above earth, however nobly he walked it. The little fragile creature had wings; and he could expand them at will, and ascend, if to no great imaginative height, yet to charming fairy circles just above those of the world about him, disclosing enchanting visions at the top of drawing-rooms, and enabling us to see the spirits that wait on coffee-cups and hoop-petticoats. [1]

## AN EVENING WITH POPE. [2]

[From "Family Journal," No. 7, June, 1825. "The New Monthly Magazine." "London Journal," Sept. 5th, 1835. "Table Talk," 1851. C. Kent, 1889.]

July 4th, 1727.

YESTERDAY was a day of delight. I dined with Mr. Pope. The only persons present were the venerable lady his mother, Mrs. Martha Blount, and Mr. Walscott, a great Tory, but as great a lover of

[1] See also "Conversations of Pope and Swift" at the end of "Table Talk," and the next essay.—ED.

[2] Supposed to have been written by Aspley Honeycomb, nephew of the "Simon Honeycomb, who wrote a letter to the *Spectator* (No. 154), which put Will into a great taking." The whole "Family Journal" is edited by one Harry H., "the lineal descendant of the famous Will Honeycomb, of 'Spectator' [Sir Roger de Coverley] memory."—ED.

Dryden ; which Mr. Pope was pleased to inform me was the reason he had invited me to meet him. Mr. Pope was in black, with a tie-wig. I could not help regarding him, as he sat leaning in his armchair before dinner, in the light of a portrait for posterity. When he came into the room, after kindly making me welcome, he took some flowers out of a little basket that he had brought with him, and presented them, not to Mrs. Martha, who I thought looked as if she expected it, but to Mrs. Pope ; which I thought very pretty and like a gentleman, not in the ordinary way. But the other had no reason to be displeased ; for turning to her with the remainder, he said, " I was thinking of a compliment to pay you ; so I have done it." He flatters with as much delicacy as Sir Richard Steele ; and the ladies like it as much from him. What fine-shaped fellows have I seen, who could not call up half such looks into their eyes !

# GRAY.

## [BORN 1716—DIED 1771.]

[Put together from the prefaces to various extracts from Gray in " Book for a Corner," 1849.]

G RAY appears to us to be the best letter-writer in the language. Others equal him in particular qualities, and surpass him in amount of entertainment ; but none are so nearly faultless. Chesterfield wants heart, and even his boasted " delicacy ;" Bolingbroke and

Pope want simplicity ; Cowper is more lively than strong ; Shenstone reminds you of too many rainy days, Swift of too many things which he affected to despise, Gibbon too much of the formalist and *littérateur*. The most amusing of all our letter-writers are Horace Walpole and Lady Mary Wortley Montagu ; but though they had abundance of wit, sense, and animal spirits, you are not always sure of their veracity. Now, the " first quality in a companion," as Sir William Temple observes, " is truth ; " and Gray's truth is as manifest as his other good qualities. He has sincerity, modesty, manliness (in spite of a somewhat effeminate body), learning, good-nature, playfulness, a perfect style ; and if an air of pensiveness breathes over all, it is only of that resigned and contemplative sort which completes our sympathy with the writer. . . .

Gray is the " melancholy Jacques " of English literature, without the sullenness or causticity. His melancholy is of the diviner sort of Milton and Beaumont, and is always ready to assume a kindly cheerfulness. . . . [His] Ode on a distant prospect of Eton College . . . . is full of thought, tenderness, and music, and should make the writer beloved by all persons of reflection, especially those who know what it is to visit the scenes of their schooldays. They may not all regard them in the same melancholy light ; but the melancholy light will cross them, and then Gray's lines will fall in upon the recollection, at once like a bitter and a balm. . . . We desire to say as little as possible about this affecting and noble poem [the " Elegy in a Country

Churchyard "]. It is so sweet, so true, and so universally appreciated, that we feel inclined to be as silent before it, as if listening to the wind over the graves. . . .

[It] is as sweet as if written by Coleridge, and as pious and universal as if religion had uttered it, undisturbed by polemics. It is a quintessence of humanity.

# GOLDSMITH.[1]
## [BORN 1728—DIED 1774.]

[From the Essay on Goldsmith in "Classic Tales," 1806.]

IF Goldsmith were characterized in a few words, I would describe him as a writer generally original, yet imitative of the best models ; from these he gathered all the chief qualities of style, and became elegant and animated in his language ; while from experience [2] rather than from books he obtained his knowledge, and became natural and original in his thoughts. His poetry has added little to English literature, because nothing that is not perfectly and powerfully original can be said to add to the poetical stock of a nation ; but his prose exhibits this quality in the highest degree : if he was more

---

[1] See also essay in "Wit and Humour."—Ed.

[2] "Experience, which is the logic of fact." See another part of the same essay.

of the humourist than the wit, it was not for want of invention ; humour was the familiar delight, wit the occasional exercise of his genius. In short, he was one of those happy geniuses who are welcome to a reader in every frame of mind, for his seriousness and his gaiety are equally unaffected and equally instructive.

# BURNS.

## [BORN 1759—DIED 1796.]

[" Jar of Honey from Mount Hybla," 1847. Reprinted from " Ainsworth's Magazine," 1844.]

HE [Burns] was pastoral poetry itself, in the shape of an actual, glorious peasant, vigorous as if Homer had written him, and tender as generous strength or as memories of the grave. Ramsey .... is but a small part of Burns—is but a field in a corner compared with 'the whole Scots pastoral region. He has none of Burns' pathos ; none of his grandeur ; none of his burning energy ; none of his craving after universal good. How universal is Burns ! What mirth in his cups ! What softness in his tears ! What sympathy in his very satire ! What manhood in everything ! If Theocritus, the inventor of a loving and affecting Polyphemus, could have foreseen the verses on the " Mouse " and the " Daisy " turned up with the plough, the " Tam o' Shanter," " O Willie brew'd a peck o' maut,"

" Ye Banks and Braes o' bonnie Doon," &c. (not to mention a hundred others, which have less to do with our subject), tears of admiration would have rushed into his eyes.

# WORDSWORTH.

## [BORN 1770—DIED 1850.]

[From the Preface to the second edition of " The Feast of the Poets," July 11th, 1815.]

**T**HE author does not scruple to confess, that his admiration of him [Wordsworth] has become greater and greater between every publication of " The Feast of the Poets." [1] He has become a convert, not indeed to what he still considers as his faults, but, to use a favourite phrase of these times, to the " immense majority " of his beauties ;—and here, it seems to him, lies the great mistake, which certain intelligent critics persist in sharing with others of a very different description. It is to be observed by the way, that the defects of Mr. Wordsworth are the result of theory, not incapacity ; and it is with their particular effect on those most calculated to understand him that we quarrel, rather than with anything else. But taking him as a mere author to be criticised, the writers in question seem to regard him as a stringer of puerilities, who has so many faults that you can only wonder now and then at

[1] This being the third. It appeared first in " The Reflector," 1811.—ED.

his beauties ; whereas the proper idea of him is that of a noble poet, who has so many beauties that you are only apt now and then, perhaps with no great wisdom, to grow impatient at his faults.

# COLERIDGE.

## [BORN 1773—DIED 1834.]

**["Imagination and Fancy," 1844. C. Kent, 1889.]**

COLERIDGE lived in the most extraordinary and agitated period of modern history ; and to a certain extent he was so mixed up with its controversies, that he was at one time taken for nothing but an apostate republican, and at another for a dreaming theosophist. The truth is, that both his politics and theosophy were at the mercy of a discursive genius, intellectually bold but educationally timid, which, anxious, or rather willing, to bring conviction and speculation together, mooting all points as it went, and throwing the subtlest glancing lights on many, ended in satisfying nobody, and concluding nothing. Charles Lamb said of him, that he had "the art of making the unintelligible appear intelligible." He was the finest dreamer, the most eloquent talker, and the most original thinker of his day ; but for want of complexional energy, did nothing with all the vast *prose* part of his mind but help the Germans to give a subtler tone to criticism, and sow a few valuable seeds of thought in minds worthy to receive them. Nine-

tenths of his theology would apply equally well to
their own creeds in the mouths of a Brahmin or a
Mussulman.

His poetry is another matter.   It is so beautiful,
and was so quietly content with its beauty, making
no call on the critics, and receiving hardly any
notice, that people are but now beginning to awake
to a full sense of its merits.  Of pure poetry, strictly
so called, that is to say, consisting of nothing but
its essential self, without conventional and perishing helps, he was the greatest master of his time.
If you could see it in a phial, like a distillation of
roses (taking it, I mean, at its best), it would be
found without a speck.   The poet is happy with
so good a gift, and the reader is " happy in his
happiness."   Yet so little, sometimes, are a man's
contemporaries and personal acquaintances able or
disposed to estimate him properly,   that while
Coleridge, unlike Shakespeare, lavished praises on
his poetic friends, he had all the merit of the generosity to himself ; and even Hazlitt, owing perhaps
to causes of political alienation, could see nothing
to admire in the exquisite poem of " Christabel,"
but the description of the quarrel between the
friends !   After speaking, too, of the " Ancient
Mariner " as the only one of his poems that he
could point out to anyone as giving an adequate
idea of his great natural powers, he adds, " It is
High German, however, and in it he seems to
conceive of poetry but as a drunken dream, reck-
less, careless, and heedless of past, present, and to
come."   This is said of a poem, with which fault
has been found for the exceeding conscientiousness

of its moral ! O ye critics, the best of ye, what havoc does personal difference play with your judgments ! It was not Mr. Hazlitt's only or most unwarrantable censure, or one which friendship found hardest to forgive. But peace, and honour too, be with his memory ! If he was a splenetic and sometimes jealous man, he was a disinterested politician and an admirable critic : and lucky were those whose natures gave them the right and the power to pardon him.

Coleridge, though a born poet, was in his style and general musical feeling the disciple partly of Spenser, and partly of the fine old English ballad-writers in the collection of Bishop Percy. But if he could not improve on them in some things, how he did in others, especially in the art of being thoroughly musical ! Of all our writers of the briefer narrative poetry, Coleridge is the finest since Chaucer ; and assuredly he is the sweetest of all our poets. Waller's music is but a court-flourish in comparison ; and though Beaumont and Fletcher, Collins, Gray, Keats, Shelley, and others, have several as sweet passages, and Spenser is in a certain sense musical throughout, yet no man has written whole poems, of equal length, so perfect in the sentiment of music, so varied with it, and yet leaving on the ear so unbroken and single an effect.

> *A damsel with a dulcimer*
> *In a vision once I saw ;*
> *It was an Abyssinian maid,*
> *And on her dulcimer she play'd,*
> *Singing of Mount Abora.*

*That* is but one note of a music ever sweet, yet never cloying. . . .

We see how such a poet obtains his music. Such forms of melody can proceed only from the most beautiful inner spirit of sympathy and imagination. He sympathizes, in his universality, with antipathy itself. If Regan or Goneril had been a young and handsome witch of the times of chivalry; and at-tuned her violence to craft, or betrayed it in veno-mous looks, she could not have beaten the soft-voiced, appalling spells, or sudden, snake-eyed glances of the Lady Geraldine,—looks which the innocent Christabel, in her fascination, feels com-pelled to " imitate." . . .

Oh ! it is too late now ; and habit and self-love blinded me at the time, and I did not know (much as I admired him) how great a poet lived in that grove at Highgate ; or I would have cultivated its walks more, as I might have done, and endeavoured to return him, with my gratitude, a small portion of the delight his verses have given me.

I must add, that I do not think Coleridge's earlier poems at all equal to the rest. Many, in-deed, I do not care to read a second time ; but there are some ten or a dozen, of which I never tire, and which will one day make a small and precious volume to put in the pockets of all enthu-siasts in poetry, and endure with the language. Five of these are " The Ancient Mariner," " Chris-tabel," " Kubla Khan," " Geneviève," and " Youth and Age." Some, that more personally relate to the poet, will be added for the love of him, not omitting the " Visit of the Gods," from Schiller, and the famous passage on the Heathen Mythology, also from Schiller. A short life, a portrait, and some other engravings perhaps, will complete the book, after the good old fashion of Cooke's and Bell's editions of the Poets ; and then, like the contents of the Jew of Malta's casket, there will be

Infinite riches in a little room.[1]


# CHARLES LAMB.[2]
## [BORN 1775—DIED 1834.]

[" Lord Byron and his Contemporaries," 1828. "Autobiography," 1850.]

CHARLES LAMB has a head worthy of Aristotle, with as fine a heart as ever beat in human bosom, and limbs very fragile to sustain it. There was a caricature of him sold in the shops, which pretended to be a likeness. P[rocto]r went into the shop in a passion, and asked the man what he meant by putting forth such a libel. The man apologized, and said that the artist meant no offence. Mr. Lamb's features are strongly yet delicately cut : he has a fine eye as well as forehead ; and no face carries in it greater marks of thought and feeling. It resembles that of Bacon, with less worldly vigour and more sensibility.

As his frame, so is his genius. It is as fit for

1 See also the brief memoir in "Lord Byron and his Contemporaries," reprinted in "Autobiography."—ED.
2 See also "Epistle to Charles Lamb," in vol. ii.

thought as can be, and equally as unfit for action ;
and this renders him melancholy, apprehensive,
humorous, and willing to make the best of everything as it is, both from tenderness of heart and
abhorrence of alteration.    His understanding is
too great to admit an absurdity ; his frame is not
strong enough to deliver it from a fear.    His
sensibility to strong contrasts is the foundation of
his humour, which is that of a wit at once melancholy and willing to be pleased.  ' He will beard a
superstition, and shudder at the old phantasm
while he does it.    One could imagine him cracking
a jest in the teeth of a ghost, and then melting into
thin air himself, out of sympathy with the awful.
His humour and his knowledge both, are those of
Hamlet, of Molière, of Carlin, who shook a city
with laughter, and, in order to divert his melancholy, was recommended to go and hear himself.
Yet he extracts a real pleasure out of his jokes,
because good-heartedness retains that privilege,
when it fails in everything else.    I should say he
condescended to be a punster, if condescension
were a word befitting wisdom like his.    Being told
that somebody had lampooned him, he said, "Very
well, I'll Lamb-pun him."    His puns are admirable, and often contain as deep things as the
wisdom of some who have greater names.    Such a
man, for instance, as Nicole, the Frenchman,
was a baby to him.    He would have cracked a
score of jokes at him, worth his whole book of
sentences ; pelted his head with pearls.    Nicole
would not have understood him, but Rochefoucault
would, and Pascal too ; and some of our old Eng-

lishmen would have understood him still better.
He would have been worthy of hearing Shakespeare read one of his scenes to him, hot from the
brain. Commonplace finds a great comforter in
him, as long as it is good-natured; it is to the ill-
natured or the dictatorial only that he is startling.
Willing to see society go on as it does, because he
despairs of seeing it otherwise, but not at all agreeing in his interior with the common notions of
crime and punishment, he "*dumbfounded*" a long
tirade one evening, by taking the pipe out of
his mouth, and asking the speaker, "Whether
he meant to say that a thief was not a good
man?" To a person abusing Voltaire, and in-
discreetly opposing his character to that of Jesus
Christ, he said admirably well (though he by no
means overrates Voltaire, nor wants reverence in
the other quarter), that "Voltaire was a very good
Jesus Christ *for the French.*" He likes to see the
church-goers continue to go to church, and has
written a tale in his sister's admirable little book
("Mrs. Leicester's School") to encourage the
rising generation to do so; but to a conscientious
deist he has nothing to object; and if an atheist
found every other door shut against him, he would
assuredly not find his. I believe he would have
the world remain precisely as it is, provided it
innovated no farther; but this spirit in him is anything but a worldly one, or for his own interest.
He hardly contemplates with patience the fine new
buildings in the Regent's Park: and, privately
speaking, he has a grudge against *official* heaven-
expounders, or clergymen. He would rather, how-

ever, be with a crowd that he disliked, than feel
himself alone. He said to me one day, with a face
of great solemnity, " What must have been that
man's feelings, who thought himself *the first deist?*"
Finding no footing in certainty, he delights to confound the borders of theoretical truth and falsehood.
He is fond of telling wild stories to children, en-
grafted on things about them ; writes letters to
people abroad, telling them that a friend of theirs
[Mr. Alsager, the commercial editor of the
"Times"] has come out in genteel comedy ; and
persuaded G[eorge] D[yer] that *Lord Castlereagh*
was the author of " Waverley" ! The same excellent person walking one evening out of his friend's
house into the New River, Mr. Lamb (who was from
home at the time) wrote a paper under his signature
of Elia (now no longer anonymous), stating, that
common friends would have stood dallying on the
bank, have sent for neighbours, &c., but that *he*, in
his magnanimity, jumped in, and rescued his friend
after the old noble fashion. He wrote in the same
magazine two lives of Liston and Munden, which
the public took for serious, and which exhibit an
extraordinary jumble of imaginary facts and truth
of bye-painting. Munden he made born at " Stoke
Pogis : " the very sound of which is like the actor
speaking and digging his words. He knows how
many false conclusions and pretensions are made
by men who profess to be guided by facts only,
as if facts could not be misconceived, or figments
taken for them ; and therefore, one day, when
somebody was speaking of a person who valued
himself on being a matter-of-fact man, " Now,"

said he, " I value myself on being a matter-of-lie
man." This does not hinder his being a man of
the greatest veracity, in the ordinary sense of the
word ; but "truth," he says, "is precious, and
ought not to be wasted on everybody." Those who
wish to have a genuine taste of him, and an insight
into his modes of life, should read his essays on
" Hogarth " and " King Lear," [his " Letters,"]
his article on the " London Streets," on " Whist-
Playing," which he loves, and on " Saying Grace
before Meat," which he thinks a strange moment
to *select* for being grateful. He said once to a
brother whist-player, whose hand was more clever
than clean, and who had enough in him to afford
the joke, " M., if dirt were trumps, what hands
you would hold."


# SHELLEY.

## [BORN 1792—DIED 1822.]

[A Preface to the " Masque of Anarchy," 1832.]

\* \* \* \* \*

MR. SHELLEY'S writings have since
aided the general progress of knowledge
in bringing about a wiser period ; and
an effusion, which would have got him
cruelly misrepresented a few years back,[1] will now
do unequivocal honour to his memory, and show

---

[1] *i. e.* in 1819, when the poem was first sent to Leigh
Hunt for the " Examiner," where he did not publish it on
the ground that the people were not ready for it. —ED.

I. M

everybody what a most considerate and kind, as well as fervent heart, the cause of the world has lost.

The poem, though written purposely in a lax and familiar measure, is highly characteristical of the author. It has the usual ardour of his tone, the unbounded sensibility by which he combines the most domestic with the most remote and fanciful images, and the patience, so beautifully checking, and in fact produced by the extreme impatience of his moral feeling. His patience is the deposit of many impatiences, acting upon an equal measure of understanding and moral taste. His wisdom is the wisdom of a heart overcharged with sensibility, acquiring the profoundest notions of justice from the completest sympathy, and at once taking refuge from its pain, and working out its extremest purposes, in the adoption of a stubborn and loving fortitude which neutralizes resistance. His very strokes of humour, while they startle with their extravagance and even ghastliness, cut to the heart with pathos. The fourth and fifth stanzas, for instance, of this poem, involve an allusion which becomes affecting from our knowing what he must have felt when he wrote it. It is to his children, who were taken from him by the late Lord Chancellor, under that preposterous law by which every succeeding age might be made to blush for the tortures inflicted on the opinions of its predecessor.

"Anarchy the skeleton," riding through the streets, and grinning and bowing on each side of him,

As well as if his education
Had cost ten millions to the nation,

is another instance of the union of ludicrousness with terror. Hope, looking "more like Despair," and laying herself down before his horse's feet to die, is a touching image. The description of the rise and growth of Public Enlightenment,

—upborne on wings whose grain
Was as the light of sunny rain,

and producing "thoughts" as he went,

As stars from night's loose hair are shaken,

till on a sudden the prostrate multitude look up,

and ankle-deep in blood,
Hope, that maiden most serene,
Was walking with a quiet mien,

is rich with the author's usual treasure of imagery, and splendid words. The sixty-third[1] is a delicious[2] stanza, producing a most happy and comfort-

[1]
Science, and Poetry, and Thought,
Are thy lamps ; they make the lot
Of the dwellers in a cot
So serene, they curse it not.

[2] In another passage Leigh Hunt has taken some pains to justify this use of the word "delicious." In "Lord Byron and his Contemporaries," 1828, after speaking of James Smith (author of the "Rejected Addresses"), he says : "His brother Horace was delicious. Lord Byron used to say, that this epithet should be applied only to eatables ; and that he wondered a friend of his (I forget who) that was critical in matters of eating, should use it in any other sense. I know not what the present usage may be in the circles, but classical authority is against his lordship, from Cicero downwards ; and I am content with the modern warrant of another noble wit, the famous Lord

ing picture in the midst of visions of blood and tumult. We see the light from its cottage window. The substantial blessings of Freedom are nobly described; and, lastly, the advice given by the poet, the great national measure recommended by him, is singularly striking as a *political anticipation.* It advises what has since taken place, and what was felt by the grown wisdom of the age to be the only thing which *could* take place, with effect, as a final rebuke and nullification of the Tories; to wit, a calm, lawful, and inflexible preparation for resistance in the shape of a protesting multitude—the few against the many [1]—the laborious and suffering against the spoilt children of monopoly—Mankind against Tory-kind. It is true the poet recommends there should be no active resistance, come what might; which is a piece of fortitude, however effective, which we believe was not contemplated by the political unions : yet, in point of the spirit of the thing, the success he anticipates has actually occurred, and after his very fashion; for there really

Peterborough, who, in his fine, open way, said of Fénélon, that he was such a "delicious creature, he was forced to get away from him, else he would have made him pious!" I grant there is something in the word delicious which may be said to comprise a reference to every species of pleasant taste. It is at once a quintessence and a compound ; and a friend, to deserve the epithet, ought, perhaps, to be capable of delighting us as much over our wine, as on graver occasions. Fénélon himself could do this, with all his piety; or rather he could do it because his piety was of the true sort, and relished of everything that was sweet and affectionate."—ED.

[1] Surely a misprint for "the many against the few."—ED.

has been no resistance, except by multitudinous protest. The Tories, however desirous they showed themselves to draw their swords, did not draw them. The battle was won without a blow.

Mr. Shelley's countrymen know how anxious he was for the advancement of the coming good, but they have yet to become acquainted with his anxiety in behalf of this particular means of it— Reform. The first time I heard from him was upon the subject; it was before I knew him, and while he was a student at Oxford, in the year 1811. So early did he begin his career of philanthropy! Mankind, and their interests, were scarcely ever out of his thoughts.[1] It was a moot point, when he entered your room, whether he would begin with some half-pleasant, half-pensive joke, or quote something Greek, or ask some question about public affairs. I remember his coming upon me when I had not seen him for a long time, and after grappling my hands with both his, in his usual fervent manner, sitting down and looking at me very earnestly, with a deep though not melancholy interest in his face. We were sitting in a cottage study, with our knees to the fire, to which we had been getting nearer and nearer in the comfort of finding ourselves together; the pleasure of seeing him was my only feeling at the moment; and the air of domesticity about us was so complete, that I thought he was going to

---

[1] "Shelley, who was shocked at [the beggar's] appearance, and gave him money out of his very antipathy; for he thought nobody would help such an ill-looking person, if he did not."—"Autobiography."

speak of some family matter—either his or my own ; when he asked me, at the close of an intensity of pause, what was "the amount of the National Debt."

I used to rally him on the apparent inconsequentiality of his manner upon these occasions ; and he was always ready to carry on the joke, because he said that my laughter did not hinder me from being in earnest. With deepest love and admiration was my laughter mixed, or I should not have ventured upon paying him the compliment of it.

I have now before me his corrected proof of an anonymous pamphlet which he wrote in the year 1817, entitled " A Proposal for Putting Reform to the vote through the Country," . . . .[1] [which shows] how zealous he was on the subject ; how generous in the example which he offered to set in behalf of Reform ; and how judicious as well as fervent this most calumniated and noble spirit could be in recommending the most avowed of his opinions. The title-page of the proof is scrawled over with sketches of trees and foliage, which was a habit of his in the intervals of thinking, whenever he had pen or pencil in hand. He would indulge in it while waiting for you at an inn, or in a doorway, scratching his elms and oak-trees on the walls. He did them very spiritedly, and with what the painters [2] call a gusto, particularly in point of

[1] In the place of these dots stood a promise to give some extracts from this pamphlet, which are omitted below.—ED.

[2] Hunt had some acquaintance with the habits and talk of painters through his intimacy with West, for which see " Autobiography," p. 77.—ED.

grace. If he had room, he would add a cottage
and a piece of water, with a sailing boat mooring
among the trees. This was his *beau idéal* of a life,
the repose of which was to be earned by zeal for
his species, and warranted by the common good.
What else the image of a boat brings to the memory
of those who have lost him,[1] I will not say, especially as he is still with us in his writings. But it is
worth observing how agreeably this habit of sketch-
ing trees and bowers evinced the gentleness of my
friend's nature, the longing he had for rest, and the
smallness of his personal desires.

It has been hastily implied in a late notice of
him, in a periodical work, that he was an aristocrat
by disposition as well as birth ; a conclusion natural
enough even with intelligent men, who have been
bred among aristocratical influences ; but it is a
pity that such men should give it as their opinion,
because it tends to confirm inferior understandings
in a similar delusion, and to make the vulgarity of
would-be refinement still more confident in its
assumptions. It is acknowledged on all hands, that
Mr. Shelley's mind was not one to be measured by
common rules,—not even by such as the vulgar,
great and small, take for uncommon ones, or for
cunning pieces of corporate knowledge snugly kept
between one another. If there is anything which
I can affirm of my beloved friend, with as much
confidence as the fact of his being benevolent *and*
a friend, it is that he was totally free from mistakes
of this kind ; that he never for one moment con-

[1] For a touching account of Shelley's death and burial,
see the "Autobiography," p. 290.—ED.

founded the claims of real and essential, with those of conventional refinement ; or allowed one to be substituted for the other in his mind by any compromise of his self-love.

I will admit it to be *possible*, that there were moments in which he might have been deceived in his estimation of people's manners, in consequence of those to which he had been early accustomed ; but the charge implied against him involves a conscious or at least an habitual preference of what are called high-bred manners, for their own sakes, apart from the natures of those who exhibited them, and to the disadvantage of those to whom they had not been taught. I can affirm that it is a total mistake, and that he partook of no such weakness. I have seen him indeed draw himself up with a sort of irrepressible air of dignified objection, when moral vulgarity was betrayed in his presence, whatever might have been the rank of the betrayer ; but nobody could hail with greater joy and simplicity, or meet upon more equal grounds, the instinct of a real delicacy and good intention, come in what shape it might. Why should he have done otherwise ? He was Shelley ; and not merely a man of that name. What had ordinary high life, and its pretensions, and the getting together of a few people for the sake of giving themselves a little importance, to do with his universal affinities ? It was finely said one day in my hearing by Mr. Hazlitt, when asked why he could not temporize a little now and then, or make a compromise with an untruth, that it was " not worth his while." It was not worth Mr. Shelley's while to be an aristocrat. His spirit was large enough to take ten aristocracies into the hollow of his hand, and look at them as I have seen him look at insects from a tree, certainly with no thought of superiority or the reverse, but with a curious interest.

The quintessence of gentlemanly demeanour which was observable in Mr. Shelley, in drawing-rooms, when he was not over-thoughtful, was nothing but an exquisite combination of sense, moral grace, and habitual sympathy. It was more dignified than what is called dignity in others, because it was the heart of the thing itself, or intrinsic worth, graced by the sincerest idealism ; and not a response made by imputed merit to the homage of the imputors. The best conventional dignity could have no more come up to it than the trick of an occasion to the truth of a life.[1]

But if an aristocracy of intellect and morals were

---

[1] The consciousness of possessing the respect of others, apart from any reason for it but a conventional one, will sometimes produce a really fine expression of countenance, where the nature is good. On the other hand, I have seen Mr. Shelley, from a doubt of the sympathy of those around him, suddenly sink from the happier look above described, into an expression of misgiving and even of destitution, that was extremely touching. It arose out of a sudden impression that all the sympathy was on his side. Sympathy is undoubtedly the one thing needful and final ; and though the receipt of it on false grounds appears the most formidable obstacle in the way of its true ascendancy, and is so, yet out of the very spirit of the fact will come the salvation of the world ; for when once a right view of it gets into fashion, the prejudices as well as the understandings of mankind will be as much on that side as they are against it now, and the acceleration of good be without a drawback.

required, he was the man for one of their leaders.
High and princely was the example he could set to
an aristocracy of a different sort, as the reader
[may] see . . . . from his pamphlet. The late
death of an extraordinary man of genius, the delight
of nations, and the special glory of his country, has
just shown the blushing world what little things
could be done for him, dead or alive, by the
"great men" whom he condescended to glorify.
The manager of a Scottish theatre (to his immortal
credit)[1] has contributed, in furtherance of the
erection of a monument to him, precisely the same
sum as was drawn forth out of the money bags of
a Scottish duke in the receipt of nearly a thousand
pounds a day. . . .[2] The delight of talking about
my friend has led me into a longer preface than I
intended to write. I did not think of detaining
the reader so long from his poem : most probably,
indeed, I have not detained him. . . .[2] [I shall
not] stop to inquire how far Mr. Shelley would
have thought the feasibilities of improvement
hastened by the events that have taken place of
late years—events, one of them in particular (the
Glorious Three Days), which it would have repaid him for all his endurances had he lived to
see.

And who shall say that he has not seen them ?

---

[1] Mr. Murray. I remember the gentlemanly paternity of
his father's manner on the English stage, and the fine eyes
of his sister (Mrs. H. Siddons) ; and was not surprised to
find generosity in such a stock.

[2] Here are omitted some passages from Shelley's pamphlet.
—Ed.

For if ever there was a man upon earth, of a more spiritual nature than ordinary, partaking of the errors and perturbations of his species, but seeing and working through them with a seraphical purpose of good, such an one was Percy Bysshe Shelley.

[NOTE.—On the subject of Shelley Leigh Hunt was always roused to an enthusiasm which found many a generous expression in his published writings. "If you ask me how it is that I bear all this," he writes, in one of the saddest letters of the "Correspondence," "I answer, that I love nature and books, and think well of the capabilities of human kind. I have known *Shelley*, I have known my mother." Leigh Hunt's most lengthy notice of Shelley appeared in "Lord Byron and his Contemporaries," 1828, was reprinted in the "Autobiography," 1850, and prefixed to the "First Series" of John Camden Hotten's "Poetical Works of Percy Bysshe Shelley" (1871).—ED.]

## THE COLMAN FAMILY.[1]

[The "Edinburgh Review," July, 1841. C. Kent, 1889.]

THE only productions of Colman, besides the "Connoisseur," that have attained any stability, and are likely to keep it, are the comedies of the "Jealous Wife" and the "Clandestine Marriage." The former was written before the decease of Lord

[1] From a review under this heading of "Memoirs of the Colman Family, including their correspondence with the most distinguished Personages of their Time. By Richard Brinsley Peake." 2 vols. 8vo. London, 1841.—ED.

Bath, to whom it was dedicated ; but his lordship knew nothing of its existence, till success gave the author courage to disclose his secret. Colman was still practising at the bar, and he continued to do so, at least ostensibly, till his supposed call from it by General Pulteney ; but a compliment to Garrick, in a pamphlet, had brought him acquainted with the sovereign of the stage ; and after he had anonymously picked his way upon it, with the help of Garrick's confidence, in the farce of "Polly Honeycomb," the "Jealous Wife" was produced at Drury Lane in the month of February, 1761. It is said to have met with greater success than any new play since the "Suspicious Husband." It is at the head of what may be called comedies of negative excellence in style, and unsuperfluous truth in the action. There is no incorrectness of language, no false or forced wit, no violation of propriety of any sort ; and the plot flows as naturally onward as possible, carrying along with it a variety of amusing if not original characters, and enlivened occasionally with smart points of situation. It has been objected that the husband is too tame, and the wife too much of a termagant ; not delicate enough for the loving passion of jealousy. But jealousy is by no means always a loving passion. It is doubtless often found in connection with love ; but inasmuch as, *per se*, it is nothing but a dread of the loss of power, it has often nothing to do with love, whatever it may pretend. We have seen people who cared nothing whatsoever for their husbands and wives, very jealous of their attention to others,

purely out of the fear of the diminution of tyranni-
cal influence ; a mixed motive of a similar kind
animates perhaps a good half of ordinary jealou-
sies ; and Colman did good service against this
arrogant and worst form of the passion, by dividing
with it the better feelings of his heroine.   The
husband was also bound over to be a good deal
henpecked, in order that he might show the evil to
its full extent, as far as comedy allows.   In his
advertisement to the play, the author confessed his
obligations to Fielding, to the " Spectator," and
to the " Adelphi " of Terence ; and said that he
had received great benefit from the advice of Garrick.   The fair Mrs. George Anne Bellamy, somewhere in her Memoirs, calls him the " modern
Terence ;" and, in truth, he merited a comparison
with his favourite classic more than she was aware
of, or than he would altogether have liked to be
shown.   As Julius Cæsar, in his fine great way,
going to the heart of the matter at once, called
Terence a " half-Menander," so Colman might
have been called a half-Terence, and this comedy
adduced as the proof of it.   There is not the sen-
tentiousness of Terence ; nothing very quotable ;
there is certainly no pathos (nor is it wanted), and
the style is not eminent for expression.   But on the
other hand the language is pure and terse ; the
chief passages and situations are more sketchy than
filled up (except in Mrs. Oakley's denouncements
of her husband)—leaving a great deal to be done
by the performers ; and the characters, it must be
confessed, are faint copies of their originals.
Russet is but a small Squire Western, a dwindled

'brother of the family ; and Lord Trinket is an un-
acknowledged Lord Foppington,[1] without the
vigour even of the other's false calves. Colman
was a very little man ; diminutive, we mean, in his
person ; without the bone and muscle common to
distinguished aspirants of that class ; not one of
the Liliputian heroes recorded in Clarendon's history, and pleasantly referred to by himself in one
of his fugitive papers.[2] He was weakly and nervous. A clergyman with whom he had had a dispute (a personage very unworthy of the gentlemanly cloth of the Church of England) once gave
him a severe beating ; for which Colman very properly exhibited against him articles of the peace.
Men's physical, moral, and intellectual faculties
all hang together in more subtle connection than is
commonly supposed ; and as Terence in person
was very slender, and probably but "half a Me-
nander " in that respect as well as in comedy, so
Colman appears, every way, to have been a sort of
Terence cut down.

*       *       *       *       *

We confess we cannot feel an equal liking for his
son, George Colman "the Younger," as he delighted
to call himself. He was proud of his father, and, we
dare say, loved him as well as he could ; but such
was his total want of seriousness, that during his

---

[1] A character in Vanbrugh's "The Relapse."—ED.
[2] "The Genius," No. II., originally published in "St.
James's Chronicle," and gathered into the miscellaneous
collection called the "Connoisseur" [described as written
by "Mr. Town," a signature which Leigh Hunt himself
adopted.— ED.].

very accounts of the calamity we have just noticed,[1] he cannot help indulging in his usual jests. This is not what Yorick would have done ; nor Hamlet, with all his insight into the melancholy of mirth, have loved.

George Colman the Younger was born in the year 1762 ; educated (a little) at Westminster, Oxford, and Aberdeen (for he contrived to neutralize his father's endeavours at all three places) ; wrote his first piece in 1784; succeeded to his father's management when the latter fell ill, and to the property of the Haymarket at his death ; was fortunate enough to secure the attachment of an amiable woman and , agreeable actress (Mrs. Gibbs), whom he afterwards married ; wrote upwards of twenty pieces, chiefly for the Haymarket, in the midst of equal difficulties and jovialties ; was the author of some Peter-Pindaric tales, equally merry and indecorous ; and died in the year 1836, Examiner of Plays, and denouncer of the most harmless liberties which he himself had practised.

We do not like to find fault with him ; for though the pretensions he made to "poetry" and the serious drama were ridiculous, his conduct in the office above mentioned mercenary and provoking, and his character altogether defective as to high and estimable qualities, except gratitude to those who well treated him (which indeed is something), there must have been a good deal of stuff of some sort in a writer who could carry on a theatre, as he did for several years, almost upon the strength of

[1] Of his father going mad under unskilful medical treatment.—ED.

his own productions. Such at least is the impression upon our memory. Those who remember the Haymarket Theatre in his day, when the performances were confined to the summer-time, and what a joyous little place it was—how merrily oppressive, and how everybody went there to complain of the heat, and to forget it in the laughter—must remember the endless repetitions of the " Mountaineers," and the " Heir at Law," and the " Battle of Hexham," and the " Wags of Windsor," and " Blue Devils," and " Love Laughs at Locksmiths," and many others. Who can ever forget the sweet song and good-natured little dumpiness of Mrs. Bland ? or the straw hats and black stuff mittens of Mrs. Gibbs, with her dimpled pastoral face ? or the dry humour, covering a rich oil, of Elliston ? or the trampling, brazen-fronted onsets, and harsh, merry, grinding voice of Fawcett in Caleb Quotem ? Who did not carry away half the farces by heart, and hazard the suffocation of their families with it next morning over the breakfast-table ? And all this (let him have his due) was owing to George Colman the Younger, and his unquestioned powers of drollery and entertainment. He was not so interesting a man as his father, for he had not a particle of gravity ; and there can be no depth of sympathy where there is no serious feeling. . . . [As to his discharge of the duties of Examiner of Plays,] the secret of Colman's face-making about pretended impieties, is to be found in that want of all seriousness of feeling and belief, which turned his dramatic sentiment into cant, and his blank verse

into commonplace. He thought all gravity consisted in words. He could discern none of the
different shades of feeling which rendered the use
of a questionable word more or less proper; and
therefore the word was to be cut out at once, to
save him trouble. He was to go counter to his
own past, and, in private, existing habit; because
he had never made use of such words but in a
spirit of levity and pretension, and therefore he
thought nobody else could do otherwise. He had
also, he thought, a character to sustain—that is to
say, an official face to make; and every grimace
was to pay for the fees he had extorted in the other
part of his capacity, and show how constitutionally
he had done it; and his pecuniary difficulties were
constant, and his shame nothing; and so concluding that not to practise a "humbug" and get
money, would itself be a "humbug," and, unlike what was done by everybody else in the world,
he forgot that every new trade requires apprentice-
ship, and has its principles of decency and honour;
and plunged into an extreme of impudent inconsistency, which only exposed him to scorn and
laughter. A less licentious writer than Colman
could not have pretended to be so afraid of a little
liberty, for he does not so confound it with want
of innocence. A more pious man could not so
violently have objected to all mention of the object
of his piety; for he is in the habit of thinking about
it in ordinary, and of associating it with his pieties
towards nature, and with the affections of his
heart. To affect to shudder at the mention, on all
occasions but set and formal ones, is in truth to do

the very reverse of what is pretended; it is to turn the sentiment itself into a word instead of a feeling, and to hazard the most irreligious of all conclusions, in seeming to think that it could not be maintained but on such a condition ! And, after all, Colman himself——but the extravagance is too absurd for more comment. Never surely did clever rogue make so clumsy a mistake.

## JOHN BUNCLE.

### [" Book for a Corner," 1849.]

THE Life of John Buncle, Esq. ; containing various Observations and Reflections made in several parts of the World, and many Extraordinary Relations," is a book unlike any other in the language, perhaps in the world ; . . . John's Life is not a classic : it contains no passage which is a general favourite : no extract could be made from it of any length, to which readers of good taste would not find objections. Yet there is so curious an interest in all its absurdities ; its jumble of the gayest and gravest considerations is so founded in the actual state of things ; it draws now and then such excellent portraits from life ; and above all, its animal spirits are at once so excessive and so real, that we defy the best readers not to be entertained with it, and having had one or two specimens, not to desire more. Buncle would say, that there is " cut and come again " in him, like one of his luncheons of cold beef and a foaming tankard. . . . John is a kind of innocent Henry the Eighth of private life, without the other's fat, fury, and solemnity. He is a prodigious hand at matrimony, at divinity, at a song, at a loud " hem," and at turkey and chine. He breaks with the Trinitarians as confidently and with as much scorn as Henry did with the Pope ; and he marries seven wives, whom he disposes of by the lawful process of fever and small-pox. His book is made up of history, mathematics (literally), songs, polemics, landscapes, eating and drinking, and characters of singular men, all bound together by his introductions to and marriages with these seven successive ladies, every one of whom is a charmer, a Unitarian, and cut off in the flower of her youth. Buncle does not know how to endure her loss ; he shuts his eyes " for three days ; " is stupified ; is in despair ; till suddenly he recollects that Heaven does not like such conduct ; that it is a mourner's business ,to bow to its-decrees ; to be devout ; to be philosophic ; in short, to be jolly, and look out for another dear, bewitching partner " on Christian principles " . . . . [Most of his ladies] are discovered in lovely places reading books, and 'are always prepared for nice little suppers. . . .

It is impossible to be serious with John Buncle, Esquire, jolly dog, Unitarian, and Blue Beard ; otherwise, if we were to take him at his word, we should pronounce him, besides being a jolly dog, to be one of a very selfish description, with too good a constitution to correct him, a prodigious vanity, no feeling whatever, and a provoking contempt for everything unfortunate, or opposed to his whims. He quarrels with bigotry, and is a bigot ; with abuse, and riots in it. He hates the cruel opinions held by Athanasius, and sends people to the devil as an Arian. He kills off seven wives out of pure incontinence and love of change, yet cannot abide a rake or even the poorest victim of the rake, unless both happen to be his acquaintances. The way in which he tramples on the miserable wretches in the streets, is the very rage and triumph of hard-heartedness, furious at seeing its own vices reflected on it, unredeemed by the privileges of law, divinity, and success. But the truth is, John is no more responsible for his opinions than health itself, or a high-mettled racer. He only " thinks he's thinking." He does, in reality, nothing at all but eat, drink, talk, and enjoy himself. Amory, Buncle's creator, was in all probability an honest man, or he would hardly have been innocent enough to put such extravagance on paper. What Mrs. Amory thought of the seven wives does not appear. Probably he invented them before he knew her ; perhaps was not anxious to be reminded of them afterwards. When he was in the zenith of his health and spirits, he must have been a prodigious fellow over a bottle and beefsteak.

# MY BOOKS.[1]

["Literary Examiner," July 5th and 12th, 1823. "Indicator and Companion," 1834. A. Symons, 1888. C. Kent, 1889.]

ITTING, last winter, among my books, and walled round with all the comfort and protection which they and my fireside could afford me ; to wit, a table of high-piled books at my back, my writing-desk on one side of me, some shelves on the other, and the feeling of the warm fire at my feet ; I began to consider how I loved the authors of those books : how I loved them, too, not only for the imaginative pleasures they afforded me, but for their making me love the very books themselves, and delight to be in contact with them. I looked sideways at my Spenser, my Theocritus, and my Arabian Nights ; then above them at my Italian poets ; then behind me at my Dryden and Pope, my romances, and my Boccaccio ; then on my left side at my Chaucer, who lay on a writing-desk ; and thought how natural it was in C[harles] L[amb] to give a kiss to an old folio, as I once saw him do to Chapman's Homer. At the same time I wondered how he could sit in that front room of his with nothing but a few unfeeling tables and chairs, or at best a few engravings in trim frames, instead of putting a couple of arm-

[1] This, so far as I can discover, is the first time that this essay has been reprinted in its complete form. It was abbreviated in the volume collected from the "Indicator," and that edition has always been followed.—ED.

chairs into the back-room with the books in it, where there is but one window. Would I were there, with both the chairs properly filled, and one or two more besides ! " We had talk, Sir,"—the only talk capable of making one forget the books.

Good God ! I could cry like one of the Children in the Wood to think how far I and mine are from home ; but this would not be " decent or manly;" so I smile instead, and am philosophical enough to make your heart ache. Besides, I shall love the country I am in more and more, and on the very account for which it angers me at present.

This is confessing great pain in the midst of my books. I own it ; and yet I feel all the pleasure in them which I have expressed.

> Take me, my book-shelves, to your arms,
> And shield me from the ills of life.

No disparagement to the arms of Stella ; but in neither case is pain a reason why we should not have a high enjoyment of the pleasure.

I entrench myself in my books equally against sorrow and the weather. If the wind comes through a passage, I look about to see how I can fence it off by a better disposition of my moveables ; if a melancholy thought is importunate, I give another glance at my Spenser. When I speak of being in contact with my books, I mean it literally. I like to lean my head against them. Living in a southern climate, though in a part sufficiently northern to feel the winter, I was obliged, during that season, to take some of the books out of the study, and hang them up near the fireplace in the sitting-room,

which is the only room that has such a convenience.
I therefore walled myself in, as well as I could, in
the manner above-mentioned. I took a walk every
day, to the astonishment of the Genoese, who used
to huddle against a bit of sunny wall, like flies on
a chimney-piece ; but I did this only that I might
so much the more enjoy my *English* evening. The
fire was a wood fire instead of a coal ; but I imagined myself in the country. I remembered at the
very worst, that one end of my native land was not
nearer the other than England is to Italy.

While writing this article I am in my study
again. Like the rooms in all houses in this country
which are not hovels, it is handsome and ornamented. On one side it looks towards a garden
and the mountains; on another, to the mountains
and the sea. What signifies all this? I turn my
back upon the sea ; I shut up even one of the side
windows looking upon the mountains, and retain
no prospect but that of the trees. On the right
and left of me are book-shelves ; a bookcase is
affectionately open in front of me ; and thus kindly
inclosed with my books and the green leaves, I
write. If all this is too luxurious and effeminate,
of all luxuries it is the one that leaves you the most
strength. And this is to be said for scholarship in
general. It unfits a man for activity, for his bodily
part in the world ; but it often doubles both the
power and the sense of his mental duties ; and
with much indignation against his body, and more
against those who tyrannize over the intellectual
claims of mankind, the man of letters, like the
magician of old, is prepared " to play the devil "

with the great men of this world, in a style that astonishes both the sword and the toga.

I do not like this fine large study.  I like elegance.  I like room to breathe in, and even walk about, when I want to breathe and walk about. I like a great library next my study ; but for the study itself, give me a small snug place, almost entirely walled with books.  There should be only one window in it, looking upon trees.  Some prefer a place with few, or no books at all—nothing but a chair or a table, like Epictetus ; but I should say that these were philosophers, not lovers of books, if I did not recollect that Montaigne was both.  He had a study in a round tower, walled as aforesaid.  It is true, one forgets one's books while writing—at least they say so.  For my part, I think I have them in a sort of sidelong mind's eye ; like a second thought, which is none—like a waterfall, or a whispering wind.

I dislike a grand library to study in.  I mean an immense apartment, with books all in Museum order, especially wire-safed.  I say nothing against the Museum itself, or public libraries.  They are capital places to go to, but not to sit in ; and talking of this, I hate to read in public, and in strange company.  The jealous silence ; the dissatisfied looks of the messengers ; the inability to help yourself ; the not knowing whether you really ought to trouble the messengers, much less the Gentleman in black, or brown, who is, perhaps, half a trustee ; with a variety of other jarrings between privacy and publicity, prevent one's settling heartily to work.  They say " they manage these things better in France;" and I dare say they do; but I think I should feel still more *distrait* in France, in spite of the benevolence of the servitors, and the generous profusion of pen, ink, and paper. I should feel as if I were doing nothing but interchanging amenities with polite writers.

A grand private library, which the master of the house also makes his study, never looks to me like a real place of books, much less of authorship. I cannot take kindly to it. It is certainly not out of envy; for three parts of the books are generally trash, and I can seldom think of the rest and the proprietor together. It reminds me of a fine gentleman, of a collector, of a patron, of Gil Blas and the Marquis of Marialva; of anything but genius and comfort. I have a particular hatred of a round table (not *the* Round Table, for that was a dining one) covered and irradiated with books, and never met with one in the house of a clever man but once. It is the reverse of Montaigne's Round Tower. Instead of bringing the books around you, they all seem turning another way, and eluding your hands.

Conscious of my propriety and comfort in these matters, I take an interest in the bookcases as well as the books of my friends. I long to meddle, and dispose them after my own notions. When they see this confession, they will acknowledge the virtue I have practised. I believe I did mention his book-room to C. L., and I think he told me that he often sat there when alone. It would be hard not to believe him. His library, though not abounding in Greek or Latin (which are the only things to help some persons to an idea of literature), is anything but superficial. The depths of philosophy and poetry are there, the innermost passages of the human heart. It has some Latin too. It has also a handsome contempt for appearance. It looks like what it is, a selection made at precious intervals from the book-stalls ;—now a Chaucer at nine and twopence ; now a Montaigne or a Sir Thomas Browne at two shillings ; now a Jeremy Taylor ; a Spinoza ; an old English Dramatist, Prior, and Sir Philip Sidney ; and the books are "neat as imported." The very perusal of the backs is a " discipline of humanity." There Mr. Southey takes his place again with an old Radical friend : there Jeremy Collier is at peace with Dryden : there the lion, Martin Luther, lies down with the Quaker lamb, Sewell : there Guzman d'Alfarache thinks himself fit company for Sir Charles Grandison, and has his claims admitted. Even the "high fantastical" Duchess of Newcastle, with her laurel on her head, is received with grave honours, and not the less for declining to trouble herself with the constitutions of her maids. There is an approach to this in the library of W. C., who also includes Italian among his humanities. W[illiam] H[azlitt], I believe, has no books, except mine ; but he has Shakespeare and Rousseau by heart. [Vincent] N[ovello], who though not a bookman by profession, is fond of those who are, and who loves his volume enough to read it across the fields, has his library in the common sitting-room, which is hospitable. H. R.'s [1] books are all too modern and finely bound, which however is not his fault, for they were left him by will,—not the most

---

[1] Henry Robinson, the treasurer of Cove nt Garden Theatre. (A. Symons, p. 313.)

kindly act of the testator. Suppose a man were to bequeath us a great japan chest three feet by four, with an injunction that it was always to stand on the tea-table. I remember borrowing a book of H. R. which, having lost, I replaced with a copy equally well bound. I am not sure I should have been in such haste, even to return the book, had it been a common-looking volume ; but the splendour of the loss dazzled me into this ostentatious piece of propriety. I set about restoring it as if I had diminished his fortunes, and waived the privilege a friend has to use a man's things as his own. I may venture upon this ultra-liberal theory, not only because candour compels me to say that I hold it to a greater extent, with Montaigne, but because I have been a meek son in the family of book-losers. I may affirm, upon a moderate calculation, that I have lent and lost in my time (and I am eight-and-thirty), half-a-dozen decent-sized libraries,—I mean books enough to fill so many ordinary bookcases.[1] I have never complained ; and self-love, as well as gratitude, makes me love those who do not complain of me.

But, like other patient people, I am inclined to burst out now that I grow less strong,—now that writing puts a hectic to my cheek. Publicity is nothing nowadays "between friends." There is R., not H. R., who in return for breaking my set of English Poets, makes a point of forgetting me, whenever he has poets in his eye ; which is carrying his conscience too far. But W[illiam] H[azlitt] treated me worse ; for not content with losing other

[1] See "A Shelf of Old Books," by Mrs. Fields, in " Scribner's Magazine " for March, 1888, p. 292.—Ed.

of said English Poets, together with my Philip Sidney (all in one volume) and divers pieces of Bacon, he vows I never lent them to him ; which is " the unkindest cut of all." This comes of being magnanimous. It is a poor thing after all to be "pushed from a level consideration" of one's superiority in matters of provocation. But W[illiam] H[azlitt] is not angry on this occasion though he is forgetful ; and in spite of his offences against me and mine (not to be done away with by his good word at intervals), I pardon the irritable patriot and metaphysician, who would give his last penny to an acquaintance, and his last pulse to the good of mankind. Why did he fire up at an idle word from one of the few men,[1] who thought as deeply as himself, and who "died daily" in the same awful cause? But I forgive him, because *he* forgave him, and yet I know not if I can do it for that very reason.

> " Come, my best friends, my books, and lead me on :
> 'Tis time that I were gone."

I own I borrow books with as much facility as I lend. I cannot see a work that interests me on another person's shelf, without a wish to carry it off : but, I repeat, that I have been much more sinned against than sinning in the article of nonreturn ; and am scrupulous in the article of intention. I never had a felonious intent upon a book but once ; and then I shall only say, it was under circumstances so peculiar, that I cannot but look upon the conscience that induced me to restore it, as having sacrificed the spirit of its very self to the letter ; and I have a grudge against it accordingly.

[1] No doubt Shelley.—ED.

Some people are unwilling to lend their books. I have a special grudge against them, particularly those who accompany their unwillingness with uneasy professions to the contrary, and smiles like Sir Fretful Plagiary. The friend who helped to spoil my notions of property, or rather to make them too good for the world "as it goes," taught me also to undervalue my squeamishness in refusing to avail myself of the books of these gentlemen. He showed me how it was doing good to all parties to put an ordinary face on the matter ; though I know his own blushed not a little sometimes in doing it, even when the good to be done was for another. (Dear S[helley], in all thy actions, small as well as great, how sure was the beauty of thy spirit to break forth.) I feel, in truth, that even when anger inclines me to exercise this privilege of philosophy, it is more out of revenge than contempt. I fear that in allowing myself to borrow books, I sometimes make extremes meet in a very sinful manner, and do it out of a refined revenge. It is like eating a miser's beef at him.

I yield to none in my love of bookstall urbanity. I have spent as happy moments over the stalls (until the woman looked out), as any literary apprentice boy who ought to be moving onwards. But I confess my weakness in liking to see some of my favourite purchases neatly bound. The books I like to have about me most are, Spenser, Chaucer, the minor poems of Milton, the Arabian Nights, Theocritus, Ariosto, and such old good-natured speculations as Plutarch's Morals. For most of these I like a plain good old binding, never mind

how old, provided it wears well ; but my Arabian
Nights may be bound in as fine and flowery a
style as possible, and I should love an engraving
to every dozen pages.  Book-prints of all sorts,
bad and good, take with me as much as when I
was a child : and I think some books, such as
Prior's Poems, ought always to have portraits of
the authors.   Prior's airy face with his cap on, is
like having his company.   From early association,
no edition of Milton pleases me so much, as that
in which there are pictures of the Devil with brute
ears, dressed like a Roman General : nor of Bun-
yan, as the one containing the print of the Valley
of the Shadow of Death, with the Devil whispering
in Christian's ear, or old Pope by the way side, and

Vanity Fair,
With the Pilgrims suffering there.

I delight in the recollection of the puzzle I used to
have with the frontispiece of the " Tale of a Tub,"
of my real horror at the sight of that crawling old
man representing Avarice, at the beginning of
" Enfield's Speaker," the " Looking Glass," or
some such book ; and even of the careless schoolboy hats, and the prim stomachers and cottage
bonnets, of such golden-age antiquities as the
" Village School."   The oldest and most worn-
out woodcut, representing King Pippin, Goody
Two Shoes, or the grim Soldan, sitting with three
staring blots for his eyes and mouth, his sceptre in
one hand, and his other five fingers raised and
spread in admiration at the feats of the Gallant
London Prentice, cannot excite in me a feeling of
ingratitude.   Cooke's edition of the British Poets

and Novelists came out when I was at school : for which reason I never could put up with Suttaby's or Walker's publications, except in the case of such works as the " Fairy Tales," which Mr. Cooke did not publish. Besides, they are too cramped, thick, and mercenary ; and the pictures are all frontispieces. They do not come in at the proper places. Cooke realized the old woman's *beau ideal* of a prayer-book,—" A little book, with a great deal of matter, and a large type : "— for the type was really large for so small a volume. Shall I ever forget his Collins and his Gray, books at once so "superbly ornamented " and so inconceivably cheap ? Sixpence could procure much before ; but never could it procure so much as then, or was at once so much respected, and so little cared for. His artist Kirk was the best artist, except Stothard, that ever designed for periodical works ; and I will venture to add (if his name rightly announces his country) the best artist Scotland ever produced, except Wilkie, but he unfortunately had not enough of his country in him to keep him from dying young. His designs for Milton and the Arabian Nights, his female extricated from the water in the " Tales of the Genii," and his old hag issuing out of the chest of the Merchant Abadah in the same book, are before me now, as vividly as they were then. He possessed elegance and the sense of beauty in no ordinary degree ; though they sometimes played a trick or so of foppery. I shall never forget the gratitude with which I received an odd number of Akenside, value sixpence, one of the set of that poet, which a boarder distributed among three or four of us, " with his mother's compliments. " The present might have been more lavish, but I hardly thought of that. I remember my number. It was the one in which there is a picture of the poet on a sopha, with Cupid coming to him, and the words underneath, " Tempt me no more, insidious Love ! " The picture and the number appeared to me equally divine. I cannot help thinking to this day, that it is right and natural in a gentleman to sit in a stage dress, on that particular kind of sopha, though on no other, with that exclusive hat and feathers on his head, telling Cupid to begone with a tragedy air. Cowley says that even when he was " a very young boy at school, instead of his running about on holidays, and playing with his fellows, he was wont to steal from them and walk into the fields, either alone with a book, or with some one companion, if he could find one of the same temper." When I was at school, I had no fields to run into, or I should certainly have gone there ; and I must own to having played a great deal ; but then I drew my sports as much as possible out of books, playing at Trojan wars, chivalrous encounters with coal-staves, and even at religious mysteries. When I was not at these games, I was either reading in a corner, or walking round the cloisters with a book under one arm and my friend [1] linked with the other, or with my thoughts. It has since been my fate to realize all the romantic notions I had of a friend at that time, and just as I had embraced him in a distant coun-

---

[1] See poems to him in " Juvenilia."—ED.

try, to have him torn from me.[1] This it is that sprinkles the most cheerful of my speculations now with tears, and that must obtain me the reader's pardon for a style unusually chequered and egoistical. No man was a greater lover of books than he. He was rarely to be seen, unless attending to other people's affairs, without a volume of some sort, generally of Plato or one of the Greek tragedians. Nor will those who understand the real spirit of his scepticism, be surprised to hear that one of his companions was the Bible. He valued it for the beauty of some of its contents, for the dignity of others, and the curiosity of all ; though the philosophy of Solomon he thought too *Epicurean,* and the inconsistencies of other parts afflicted him. His favourite part was the book of Job, which he thought the grandest of tragedies. He projected founding one of his own upon it ; and I will undertake to say, that Job would have sat in that tragedy with a patience and profundity of thought worthy of the original. Being asked on one occasion, what book he would save for himself if he could save no other ? he answered, " The oldest book, the Bible." It was a monument to him of the earliest, most lasting, and most awful aspirations of humanity. But more of this on a fitter occasion.[2]

---

[1] Shelley again.—ED.

[2] I will mention, however, in this place, that an advantage of a very cunning and vindictive nature was taken of Mr. Shelley's known regard for the Bible, to represent him as having one with him at the time he was drowned. Nothing was more probable ; and it is true that he had a book in his pocket, the remains of which, at the request of the author of this article, were buried with him, but it was the volume of

I. O

[1] I love an author the more for having been him-self a lover of books. The idea of an ancient library perplexes our sympathy by its map-like volumes, rolled upon cylinders. Our imagination cannot take kindly to a yard of wit, or to thirty inches of moral observation, rolled out like linen in a draper's shop. But we conceive of Plato as of a lover of books ; of Aristotle certainly ; of Plutarch, Pliny, Horace, Julian, and Marcus Aurelius. . Virgil, too, must have been one ; and, after a fashion, Martial. May I confess, that the passage which I recollect with the greatest plea-sure in Cicero, is where he says that books delight us at home, *and are no impediment abroad ;* travel with us, ruralize with us. His period is rounded off to some purpose : "*Delectant domi, non impe-diunt foris ; peregrinantur, rusticantur.*" I am so much of this opinion, that I do not care to be anywhere without having a book or books at hand, and like Dr. Orkborne, in the novel of "Camilla," stuff the coach or post-chaise with them whenever I travel. As books, however, become ancient, the love of them becomes more unequivocal and con-spicuous. The ancients had little of what we call learning. They made it. They were also no very eminent buyers of books—they made books for posterity. It is true, that it is not at all necessary

Mr. Keats' poems, containing "Hyperion," of which he was a great admirer. He borrowed it of me when I went away, and knowing how I valued it also, said that he would not let it quit him till he saw me again.

[1] This is the beginning of the second article of July 12th. —ED.

to love many books, in order to love them much.
The scholar, in Chaucer, who would rather have

**At his beddes head**
**A twenty bokes, clothed, in black and red,**
**Of Aristotle and his philosophy,**
**Than robès rich, or fiddle, or psaltry—**

doubtless beat all our modern collectors in his
passion for reading ; but books must at least exist,
and have acquired an eminence, before their lovers
can make themselves known. There must be a
possession, also, to perfect the communion ; and
the mere contact is much, even when our mistress
speaks an unknown language. Dante puts Homer,
the great ancient, in his Elysium, upon trust ;
but a few years afterwards, "Homer," the book,
made its appearance in Italy, and Petrarch, in a
transport, put it upon his book-shelves, where he
adored it, like "the unknown God." Petrarch
ought to be the god of the Bibliomaniacs, for he
was a collector and a man of genius, which is an
union that does not often happen. He copied out,
with his own precious hand, the manuscripts he
rescued from time, and then produced others for
time to reverence. With his head upon a book he
died. Boccaccio, his friend, was another ; nor can
one look upon the longest and most tiresome works
he wrote (for he did write some tiresome ones, in
spite of the gaiety of his "Decameron"), without
thinking, that in that resuscitation of the world of
letters, it must have been natural to a man of
genius to add to the existing stock of volumes, at
whatsoever price. I always pitch my completest

idea of a lover of books, either in these dark ages, as they are called,

(Cui cieco a torto il cieco volgo appella—)

or in the gay town days of Charles II., or a little afterwards.   In both times the portrait comes out by the force of contrast.   In the first, I imagine an age of iron warfare and energy, with solitary re-treats, in which the monk or the hooded scholar walks forth to meditate, his precious volume under his arm.   In the other, I have a triumphant example of the power of books and wit to contest the victory with sensual pleasure :—Rochester, staggering home to pen a satire in the style of Monsieur Boileau ; Butler, cramming his jolly duodecimo with all the learning that he laughed at ; and a new race of book poets come up, who, in spite of their periwigs and petit-maîtres, talk as romantically of "the bays," as if they were priests of Delphos.   It was a victorious thing in books to beguile even the old French of their egotism, or at least to share it with them.   Nature never pre-tended to do as much.   And here is the difference between the two ages, or between any two ages in which genius and art predominate.   In the one, books are loved because they are the records of nature and her energies ; in the other, because they are the records of those records, or evidences of the importance of the individuals, and proofs of our descent in the new and imperishable aristo-cracy.   This is the reason why rank (with few ex-ceptions) is so jealous of literature, and loves to appropriate or withhold the honours of it, as if

they were so many toys and ribbons, like its own.
It has an instinct that the two pretensions are incompatible. When Montaigne (a real lover of
books) affected the order of St. Michael, and
pleased himself with possessing that fugitive little
piece of importance, he did it because he would
pretend to be above nothing that he really felt, or
that was felt by men in general ; but at the same
time he vindicated his natural superiority over this
weakness by praising and loving all higher and
lasting things, and by placing his best glory in
doing homage to the geniuses that had gone before
him. · He did not endeavour to think that an immortal renown was a fashion, like that of the cut
of his scarf ; or that by undervaluing the one,
he should go shining down to posterity in the
other, perpetual lord of Montaigne and of the
ascendant.

There is a period of modern times, at which the
love of books appears to have been of a more decided nature than at either of these—I mean the
age just before and after the Reformation, or
rather all that period when book-writing was confined to the learned languages. Erasmus is the
god of it. Bacon, a mighty book-man, saw, among
his other sights, the great advantage of loosening
the vernacular tongue, and wrote both Latin and
English. I allow this is the greatest closeted age
of books ; of old scholars sitting in dusty studies ;
of heaps of " illustrious obscure," rendering themselves more illustrious and more obscure by retreat-
ing from the " thorny queaches " of Dutch and
German names into the " vacant interlunar caves "

of appellations latinized or translated.   I think I
see all their volumes now, filling the shelves of a
dozen German convents.   The authors are bearded
men, sitting in old woodcuts, in caps and gowns,
and their books are dedicated to princes and states-
men, as illustrious as themselves.   My old friend
Wierus, who wrote a thick book, " De Præstigiis
Dæmonum," was one of them, and had a fancy
worthy of his sedentary stomach.   I will confess,
once for all, that I have a liking for them all.   It
is my link with the bibliomaniacs, whom I admit
into our relationship, because my love is large, and
my family pride nothing.   But still I take my idea
of books read with a gusto, of companions for bed
and board, from the two ages before-mentioned.
The other is of too book-worm a description.
There must be both a judgment and a fervour ; a
discrimination and a boyish eagerness ; and (with
all due humility) something of a point of contact
between authors worth reading and the reader.
How can I take Juvenal into the fields, or Val-
carenghius " De Aortæ Aneurismate " to bed
with me ?   How could I expect to walk before
the face of nature with the one ; to tire my elbow
properly with the other, before I put out my
candle, and turn round deliciously on the right
side ?   Or how could I stick up Coke upon
Littleton against something on the dinner-table,
and be divided between a fresh paragraph and a
mouthful of salad ?

I take our four great English poets to have all
been fond of reading.   Milton and Chaucer pro-
claim themselves for hard sitters at books.   Spen-

ser's reading is evident by his learning; and if there were nothing else to show for it in Shakespeare, his retiring to his native town, long before old age, would be a proof of it. It is impossible for a man to live in solitude without such assistance, unless he is a metaphysician or mathematician, or the dullest of mankind; and any country town would be solitude to Shakespeare, after the bustle of a metropolis and a theatre. Doubtless he divided his time between his books, and his bowling-green, and his daughter Susanna. It is pretty certain, also, that he planted, and rode on horseback; and there is evidence of all sorts to make it clear, that he must have occasionally joked with the blacksmith, and stood godfather for his neighbours' children. Chaucer's account of himself must be quoted, for the delight and sympathy of all true readers :—

> And as for me, though that I can but lite,
> On bookès for to rede I me delite,
> And to hem yeve I faith and full credènce,
> And in mine herte have hem in reverence
> So hertèly, that there is gamè none,
> That fro my bookès maketh me to gòne,
> But it is seldome on the holy daie ;
> Save certainly whan that the month of May
> Is comen, and that I hear the foulès sing,
> And that the flourès ginnen for to spring.
> Farewell my booke and my devociõn.
> > *The Legend of Good Women.*

And again, in the second book of his " House of Fame," where *the eagle* addresses him :—

> ———Thou wilt make
> At night full oft thine head to ake,

And in thy study as thou writest,
And evermore of Love enditest,
In honour of him and his praisings,
And in his folkès furtherings,
And in his matter all devisest,
And not him ne his folke despisest,
Although thou mayst go in the daunse
Of hem, that him list not advance ;
Therefore as I said, ywis,
Jupiter considreth well this.
And also, beausire, of other things ;
That is, thou hast no tidings
Of Lovès folke, if they be glade,
Ne of nothing else that God made,
And not only fro ferre countree,
But no tidings commen to thee,
Not of thy very neighbouris,
That dwellen almost at thy dores ;
Thou hearest neither that ne this,
For whan thy labour all done is,
And hast made all thy rekenings,[1]
Instead of rest and of new things,
Thou goest home to thine house anone,
And all so dombe as anie stone,
Thou sittest at another booke,
Till fully dazed is thy looke.

After I think of the bookishness of Chaucer and Milton, I always make a great leap to Prior and Fenton. Prior was first noticed, when a boy, by Lord Dorset, sitting in his uncle's tavern, and reading Horace. He describes himself, years after, when Secretary of Embassy at the Hague, as taking the same author with him in the Saturday's chaise, in which he and his mistress used to escape from town cares into the country, to the

[1] Chaucer at this time had an office under the government.

admiration of Dutch beholders. Fenton was a
martyr to contented scholarship (including a sir-
loin and a bottle of wine), and died among his
books, of inactivity. "He rose late," says Johnson, "and when he had risen, sat down to his
books and papers." A woman that once waited
on him in a lodging, told him, as she said, that he
would "lie a-bed and be fed with a spoon." He
must have had an enviable liver, if he was happy.
I must own (if my conscience would let me), that
I should like to lead, half the year, just such a life
(woman included, though not that woman), the
other half being passed in the fields and woods,
with a cottage just big enough to hold us. Dacier
and his wife had a pleasant time of it ; both fond
of books, both scholars, both amiable, both wrapt
up in the ancient world, and helping one another
at their tasks. If they were not happy, matrimony
would be a rule even without an exception. Pope
does not strike me as being a book-man ; he was
curious rather than enthusiastic ; more nice than
wise ; he dabbled in modern Latin poetry, which
is a bad symptom. Swift was decidedly a reader ;
the "Tale of a Tub," in its fashion as well as sub-
stance, is the work of a scholarly wit ; the "Battle
of the Books" is the fancy of a lover of libraries.
Addison and Steele were too much given up to
Button's and the town. Periodical writing, though
its demands seem otherwise, is not favourable to
reading ; it becomes too much a matter of business,
and will either be attended to at the expense of the
writer's books, or books, the very admonishers of
his industry, will make him idle. Besides, a

periodical work, to be suitable to its character,
and warrant its regular recurrence, must involve
something of a gossiping nature, and proceed upon
experiences familiar to the existing community, or
at least likely to be received by them in consequence of some previous tinge of inclination. You
do not pay weekly visits to your friends to lecture
them, whatever good you may do their minds.
There will be something compulsory in reading
the " Ramblers," as there is in going to church.
Addison and Steele undertook to regulate the
minor morals of society, and effected a world of
good, with which scholarship had little to do.
Gray was a book-man ; he wished to be always
lying on sofas, reading "eternal new novels of
Crebillon and Marivaux." This is a true hand.
The elaborate and scientific look of the rest of his
reading was owing to the necessity of employing
himself : he had not health and spirits for the
literary voluptuousness he desired. Collins, for
the same reason, could not employ himself ; he
was obliged to dream over Arabian tales, to let the
light of the supernatural world half in upon his
eyes. " He loved," as Johnson says (in that strain
of music, inspired by tenderness), " fairies, genii,
giants, and monsters ; he delighted to rove through
the meanders of enchantment, to gaze on the
magnificence of golden palaces, to repose by the
waterfalls of Elysian gardens." If Collins had had
a better constitution, I do not believe that he
would have written his projected work upon the
" Restoration of Literature," fit as he was by
scholarship for the task, but he would have been

the greatest poet since the days of Milton. If his friend Thomas Warton had had a little more of his delicacy of organization, the love of books would almost have made him a poet. His edition of the minor poems of Milton is a wilderness of sweets. It is the only one in which a true lover of the original can pardon an exuberance of annotation; though I confess I am inclined enough to pardon any notes that resemble it, however numerous. The "builded rhyme" stands at the top of the page, like a fair edifice with all sorts of flowers and fresh waters at its foot. The young poet lives there, served by the nymphs and fauns.

> Hinc atque hinc glomerantur Oreades.
> Huc ades, o formose puer : tibi lilia plenis
> Ecce ferunt nymphæ calathis : tibi candida Nais
> Pallentes violas et summa papavera carpens,
> Narcissum et florem jungit bene olentis anethi.

Among the old writers I must not forget Ben Jonson and Donne. Cowley has been already mentioned. His boyish love of books, like all the other inclinations of his early life, stuck to him to the last; which is the greatest reward of virtue. I would mention Izaak Walton, if I had not a grudge against him. His brother fishermen, the divines, were also great fishers of books. I have a grudge against them and their divinity. They talked much of the devil and divine right, and yet forgot what Shakespeare says of the devil's friend Nero, that he is "an angler in the lake of darkness." Selden was called "the walking library of our nation." It is not the pleasantest idea of him; but the library included poetry, and wit, as well as heraldry and the Jewish doctors. His "Table Talk" is equally pithy and pleasant, and truly worthy of the name, for it implies other speakers. Indeed it was actually what it is called, and treasured up by his friends. Selden wrote complimentary verses to his friends the poets, and a commentary on Drayton's "Polyolbion." Drayton was himself a reader, addicted to all the luxuries of scholarship. Chapman sat among his books, like an astrologer among his spheres and altitudes.

How pleasant it is to reflect, that all these lovers of books have themselves become books! What better metamorphosis could Pythagoras have desired! How Ovid and Horace exulted in anticipating theirs! And how the world have justified their exultation! They had a right to triumph over brass and marble. It is the only visible change which changes no farther; which generates and yet is not destroyed. Consider: mines themselves are exhausted; cities perish; kingdoms are swept away, and man weeps with indignation to think that his own body is not immortal.

> Muoiono le città, muoiono i regni,
> E l' uom d' esser mortal par che si sdegni.

Yet this little body of thought, that lies before me in the shape of a book, has existed thousands of years, nor since the invention of the press can anything short of an universal convulsion of nature abolish it. To a shape like this, so small yet so comprehensive, so slight yet so lasting, so insignificant yet so venerable, turns the mighty activity of Homer, and so turning, is enabled to live and warm us for ever. To a shape like this turns the placid sage of Academus : to a shape like this the grandeur of Milton, the exuberance of Spenser, the pungent elegance of Pope, and the volatility of Prior. In one small room, like the compressed spirits of Milton, can be gathered together ,

> The assembled souls of all that men held wise.

May I hope to become the meanest of these existences ? This is a question which every author who is a lover of books, asks himself some time in his life ; and which must be pardoned, because it cannot be helped. I know not. I cannot exclaim with the poet,

> Oh that my name were number'd among theirs,
> Then gladly would I end my mortal days.

For my mortal days, few and feeble as the rest of them may be, are of consequence to others. But I should like to remain visible in this shape. The little of myself that pleases myself, I could wish to be accounted worth pleasing others. I should like to survive so, were it only for the sake of those who love me in private, knowing as I do what a treasure is the possession of a friend's mind, when he is no more. At all events, nothing while I live and think, can deprive me of my value for such treasures. I can help the appreciation of them while I last, and love them till I die ; and perhaps, if fortune turns her face once more in kindness upon me before I go, I may chance, some quiet day, to lay my overbeating temples on a book, and so have the death I most envy.

## DEDICATION

### OF "FOLIAGE," 1818, TO SIR JOHN EDWARD SWINBURNE, BART.

My dear Sir John,

THIS book belongs to you, if you will accept it. You are not one of those who pay the strange compliment to heaven of depreciating this world, because you believe in another: you admire its beauties both in nature and art; you think that a knowledge of the finest voices it has uttered, ancient as well as modern, ought, even in gratitude, to be shared by the sex that has inspired so many of them;—a rational piety and a manly patriotism does not hinder you from putting the Phidian Jove over your organ, or flowers at the end of your room;—in short, you who visit the sick and the prisoner, for the sake of helping them without frightening, cannot look more tenderly after others, than you are regarded by your own family; nor can any one of the manly and amiable friends that I have the happiness of possessing, more fitly receive a book, the object of which is to cultivate a love of nature out of doors, and of sociality within. Pray pardon me this public compliment for my own sake, and for sincerity's. That you may long continue to be the centre of kind happy looks, and an example to the once cheerful gentry of this war and money-injured land, is the constant wish of

Your obliged

and affectionate servant,

LEIGH HUNT.

# A SCHOOLBOY'S FIRST LOVE.

["Lord Byron and his Contemporaries," 1828. "Autobiography," 1850.]

MY strolls about the fields with a book were full of happiness : only my dress used to get me stared at by the villagers. Walking one day by the little river Wandle, I came upon one of the loveliest girls I ever beheld, standing in the water with bare legs, washing some linen. She turned as she was stooping, and showed a blooming oval face with blue eyes, on either side of which flowed a profusion of flaxen locks. With the exception of the colour of the hair, it was like Raphael's own head turned into a peasant girl's. The eyes were full of gentle astonishment at the sight of me ; and mine must have wondered no less. However, I was prepared for such wonders. It was only one of my poetical visions realized, and I expected to find the world full of them. What she thought of my blue skirts and yellow stockings is not so clear. She did not, however, taunt me with my "petticoats," as the girls in the streets of London would do,[1] making me blush, as I thought they ought to have done instead. My beauty in the brook was too gentle and diffident ; at least I thought so, and my own

---

[1] "For the Christ's Hospital boy feels that he is no charity-boy . . . . in the respect, and even kindness, which his well-known garb never fails to procure him in the streets of the metropolis."—C. LAMB'S *Recollections of Christ's Hospital.*

heart did not contradict me.    I then took every
beauty for an Arcadian, and every brook for a
fairy stream ; and the reader would be surprised if
he knew to what an extent I have a similar tendency
still.    I find the same possibilities by another
path.                                                              ,

It was then that I fell in love with my cousin
Fan.    However, I would have fought all her young
acquaintances round for her, timid as I was, and
little inclined to pugnacity.                                  ,

Fanny was a lass of fifteen, with little laughing
eyes, and a mouth like a plum.    I was then (I feel
as if I ought to be ashamed to say it) not more
than thirteen, if so old ; but I had read Tooke's
" Pantheon," and came of a precocious race.    My
cousin came of one too, and was about to be married
to a handsome young fellow of three-and-twenty.    I
thought nothing of this, for nothing could be more
innocent than my intentions.    I was not old enough,
or grudging enough, or whatever it was, even to
be jealous.    I thought everybody must love Fanny
Dayrell ; and if she did not leave me out in per-
mitting it, I was satisfied.    It was enough for me
to be with her as long as I could ; to gaze on her
with delight as she floated hither and thither ; and
to sit on the stiles in the neighbouring fields, thinking of Tooke's " Pantheon."    My friendship was
greater than my love.    Had my favourite school-
fellow been ill, or otherwise demanded my return,
I should certainly have chosen his society in preference.    Three-fourths of my heart were devoted
to friendship ; the rest was in a vague dream of
beauty, and female cousins, and nymphs, and

green fields, and a feeling which, though of a
warm nature, was full of fear and respect.

Had the jade put me on the least equality of
footing as to age, I know not what change might
have been wrought in me ; but though too young
herself for the serious duties she was about to bring
on her, and full of sufficient levity and gaiety not
to be uninterested with the little black-eyed schoolboy that lingered about her, my vanity was well
paid off by hers, for she kept me at a distance by
calling me *petit garçon.* This was no better than
the assumption of an elder sister in her teens over
a younger one ; but the latter feels it, nevertheless ;
and I persuaded myself that it was particularly cruel.
. . . There would she come in her frock and tucker
(for she had not yet left off either), her curls
dancing, and her hands clasped together in the
enthusiasm of something to tell me, and when I
flew to meet her, forgetting the difference of ages,
and alive only to my charming cousin, she would
repress me with a little fillip on the cheek, and say,
" Well, *petit garçon,* what do you think of that ? "
The worst of it was, that this odious French phrase
sat insufferably well upon her plump little mouth.
She and I used to gather peaches before the house
were up. I held the ladder for her ; she mounted
like a fairy ; and when I stood doating on her as
she looked down and threw the fruit in my lap, she
would cry, " *Petit garçon,* you will let 'em all
drop ! " On my return to school, she gave me a
locket for a keepsake, in the shape of a heart ;
which was the worst thing she ever did to the *petit
garçon,* for it touched me on my weak side, and

I. P

looked like a sentiment. I believe I should have had serious thoughts of becoming melancholy, had I not, in returning to school, returned to my friend, and so found means to occupy my craving for sympathy. However, I wore the heart a long while. I have sometimes thought there was more in her French than I imagined ; but I believe not. She naturally took herself for double my age, with a lover of three-and-twenty. Soon after her marriage, fortune separated us for many years. My passion had almost as soon died away ; but I have loved the name of Fanny ever since ; and when I met her again, which was under circumstances of trouble on her part, I could not see her without such an emotion as I was fain to confess to a person "near and dear," who forgave me for it ; which is one of the reasons I have for loving the said person so well. Yes ! the "black ox" trod on the fairy foot of my light-hearted cousin Fan ; of her, whom I could no more have thought of in conjunction with sorrow, than of a ball-room with a tragedy. To know that she was rich and admired, and abounding in mirth and music, was to me the same thing as to know that she existed. How often did I afterwards wish myself rich in turn, that I might have restored to her all the graces of life ! She was generous, and would not have denied me the satisfaction.

This was my first love.

# AN ACCOUNT OF CHRIST-HOSPITAL.

["Lord Byron and his Contemporaries," 1828. "Auto-biography," 1850.]

PERHAPS there is not a foundation in the country so truly English, taking that word to mean what Englishmen wish it to mean—something solid, unpretending, of good character, and free to all. More boys are to be found in it, who issue from a greater variety of ranks, than in any school in the kingdom; and as it is the most various, so it is the largest, of all the free schools. Nobility do not go there, except as boarders. Now and then a boy of a noble family may be met with, and he is reckoned an interloper, and against the charter; but the sons of poor gentry and London citizens abound; and with them an equal share is given to the sons of tradesmen of the very humblest description, not omitting servants. I would not take my oath—but I have a very vivid recollection, that in my time there were two boys, one of whom went up into the drawing-room to his father, the master of the house; and the other, down into the kitchen to *his* father, the coachman. One thing, however, I know to be certain, and that is the noblest of all: it is, that the boys themselves (at least it was so in my time) had no sort of feeling of the difference of one another's ranks out of doors. The cleverest boy was the noblest, let his father be who he might. In short Christ-Hospital is known and respected by thousands as a nursery of tradesmen, of merchants, of naval officers, of scholars, of some of the most eminent persons of the day ; and the feeling among the boys themselves is, that it is a medium, far apart indeed, but equally so, between the patrician pretension of such schools as Eton and Westminster, and the plebeian submission of the charity schools. In point of university honours it claims to be equal with the best ; and though other schools can show a greater abundance of eminent names, I know not where will be many who are a greater host in themselves. One original author is worth a hundred transmitters of elegance : and such a one is to be found in Richardson, who here received what education he possessed. . . .

In the time of Henry VIII. Christ-Hospital was a monastery of Franciscan friars. Being dissolved among the others, Edward VI., moved by a sermon of Bishop Ridley's, assigned the revenues of it to the maintenance and education of a certain number of poor orphan children, born of citizens of London. I believe there has been no law passed to alter the letter of this intention ; which is a pity, since the alteration has taken place. An extension of it was probably very good, and even demanded by circumstances. I have reason, for one, to be grateful for it. But tampering with matters-of-fact among children is dangerous. They soon learn to distinguish between allowed poetical fiction and that which they are told, under severe penalties, never to be guilty of ; and this early sample of contradiction between the thing asserted and the obvious fact, can do no good even in an establishment so plain-dealing in other respects as Christ-Hospital.

The place is not only designated as an Orphan-house in its Latin title, but the boys, in the prayers which they repeat every day, implore the pity of heaven upon " us poor orphans." I remember the perplexity this caused me at a very early period. It is true, the word orphan may be used in a sense implying destitution of any sort ; but this was not its original meaning in the present instance; nor do the younger boys give it the benefit of that scholarly interpretation.   There was another thing (now, I believe, done away) which existed in my time, and perplexed me still more.   It seemed a glaring instance of the practice likely to result from the other assumption, and made me prepare for a hundred falsehoods and deceptions, which, mixed up with contradiction, as most things in society are, I sometimes did find, and oftener dreaded.   I allude to a foolish custom they had in the ward which I first entered, and which was the only one that the company at the public suppers were in the habit of going into, of hanging up, by the side of every bed, a clean white napkin, which was supposed to be the one used by the occupiers.   Now these napkins were only for show, the real towels being of the largest and coarsest kind.   If the masters had been asked about them, they would doubtless have told the truth ; perhaps the nurses would have done so. Bur the boys were not aware of this.   There they saw these " white lies " hanging before them, a conscious imposition ; and I well remember how alarmed I used to feel, lest any of the company should direct their inquiries to me.[1] . . .

1 " The Christ's Hospital boy's sense of right and wrong

To each of these wards [or sleeping-rooms] a
nurse was assigned, who was the widow of some
decent liveryman of London, and who had the
charge of looking after us at night-time, seeing to
our washing, &c., and carving for us at dinner :
all of which gave her a good deal of power, more
than her name warranted.   They were, however,
almost invariably very decent people, and performed
their duty ; which was not always the case with
the young ladies, their daughters.   There were five
schools ;  a grammar-school, a mathematical or
navigation-school (added by Charles II. [through
the zeal of Mr. Pepys]), a writing, a drawing, and
a reading school.   Those who could not read when
they came on the foundation, went into the last.
There were few in the last-but-one, and I scarcely
know what they did, or for what object.   The
writing-school was for those who were intended for
trade and commerce ; the mathematical, for boys
who went as midshipmen into the naval and East
India service ; and the grammar-school for such as
were designed for the Church, and to go to the
University.   The writing-school was by far the
largest ; and, what is very curious (which is not
the case now), all the schools were kept quite distinct ; so that a boy might arrive at the age of
fifteen in the grammar-school, and not know his
multiplication-table.[1] . . .

is peculiarly tender and apprehensive."—C. LAMB's *Recollections of Christ's Hospital.*
   [1] "Which was the case with L. H. himself, and the cause
of much trouble to him in after life."   See "Autobiography."

Most of these schools had several masters ; besides whom there was a steward, who took care of our subsistence, and had a general superintendence over all hours and circumstances not connected with schooling. The masters had almost all been in the school, and might expect pensions or livings in their old age. Among those in my time, the mathematical master was Mr. Wales, a man well known for his science, who had been round the world with Captain Cook ; for which we highly venerated him. He was a good man, of plain, simple manners, with a heavy large person and a benign countenance. When he was at Otaheite, the natives played him a trick while bathing, and stole his small-clothes ; which we used to think an enormous liberty, scarcely credible. The name of the steward, a thin stiff man of invincible formality of demeanour, admirably fitted to render encroachment impossible, was Hathaway.[1] We of the grammar-school used to call him "the Yeoman," on account of Shakespeare having married the daughter of a man of that name, designated as " a substantial yeoman." . . .

The persons who were in the habit of getting up in our church pulpit and reading-desk, might as well have hummed a tune to their diaphragms. They inspired us with nothing but mimicry. The name of the morning reader was Salt. He was a worthy man, I believe, and might, for aught we knew, have been a clever one ; but he had it all

[1] Charles Lamb tells a characteristic anecdote of this Mr. Hathaway, "with that patient sagacity that tempered all his conduct."

to himself. He spoke in his throat, with a sound as if he were weak and corpulent ; and was famous among us for saying " murracles " instead of "miracles." When we imitated him, this was the only word we drew upon : the rest was unintelligible suffocation. Our usual evening preacher was Mr. Sandiford, who had the reputation of learning and piety. It was of no use to us, except to make us associate the ideas of learning and piety in the pulpit with inaudible humdrum. Mr. Sandiford's voice was hollow and low ; and he had a habit of dipping up and down over his book, like a chicken drinking. Mr. Salt was eminent for a single word. Mr. Sandiford surpassed him, for he had two audible phrases. There was, it is true, no great variety in them. One was " the dispensation of Moses ; " the other (with a due interval of hum), ", the Mosaic dispensation." These he used to repeat so often, that in our caricatures of him they sufficed for an entire portrait. The reader may conceive a large church (it was Christ Church, Newgate Street), with six hundred boys, seated like charity-children up in the air, on each side of the organ, Mr. Sandiford humming in the valley, and a few maid-servants who formed his afternoon congregation. We did not dare to go to sleep. We were not allowed to read. The great boys used to get those that sat behind them to play with their hair. Some whispered to their neighbours, and the others thought of their lessons and tops. I can safely say, that many of us would have been good listeners, and most of us attentive ones, if the clergyman could have been heard. As it was, I talked as well as the rest, or thought of my exercise. Sometimes we could not help joking and laughing over our weariness; and then the fear was, lest the steward had seen us. It was part of the business of the steward to preside over the boys in church-time. He sat aloof, in a place where he could view the whole of his flock. There was a ludicrous kind of revenge we had of him, whenever a particular part of the Bible was read. This was the parable of the Unjust Steward. The boys waited anxiously till the passage commenced ; and then, as if by a general conspiracy, at the words " thou unjust steward," the whole school turned their eyes upon this unfortunate officer, who sat

> Like Teneriff or Atlas unremoved.

We persuaded ourselves, that the more uncon-scious he looked, the more he was acting. . . .

" But what is a Deputy Grecian ? " Ah, reader ! to ask that question, and at the same time to know anything at all worth knowing, would at one time, according to our notions, have been impossible. When I entered the school, I was shown three gigantic boys, young men rather (for the eldest was between seventeen and eigh-teen), who, I was told, were going to the Univer-sity. These were the Grecians. . They are the three head boys of the Grammar School, and are understood to have their destiny fixed for the Church. The next class to these, and like a College of Car-dinals to those three Popes (for every Grecian was in our eyes infallible), are the Deputy Grecians.

The former were supposed to have completed their Greek studies, and were deep in Sophocles and Euripides. The latter were thought equally competent to tell you anything respecting Homer and Demosthenes. These two classes, and the head boys of the Navigation School, held a certain rank over the whole place, both in school and out. Indeed, the whole of the Navigation School, upon the strength of cultivating their valour for the navy, and being called King's Boys,[1] had succeeded in establishing an extraordinary pretension to respect. This they sustained in a manner as laughable to call to mind as it was grave in its reception. It was an etiquette among them never to move out of a right line as they walked, whoever stood in their way. I believe there was a secret understanding with Grecians and Deputy Grecians, the former of whom were unquestionably lords paramount in point of fact, and stood and walked aloof when all the rest of the school were marshalled in bodies. I do not remember any clashing between these civil and naval powers ; but I remember well my astonishment when I first beheld some of my little comrades overthrown by the progress of one of these very straightforward [marine] personages, who walked on with as tranquil and unconscious a face as if nothing had happened. It was not a fierce-looking push ; there seemed to be no intention in it.  The insolence lay in the boy not appearing to know that such an inferior human being existed.

[1] See also C. Lamb's "Recollections of Christ's Hospital," for an account of these King's Boys, whom he calls the Janissaries of the school.

It was always thus, wherever they came. If aware, the boys got out of their way ; if not, down they went, one or more ; away rolled the top or the marbles, and on walked the future captain—

> In maiden navigation, frank and free.

They wore a badge on the shoulder, of which they were very proud; though in the streets it must have helped to confound them with charity boys. For charity boys, I must own, we all had a great contempt, or thought so. We did not dare to know that there might have been a little jealousy of our own position in it, placed as we were midway between the homeliness of the common charity-school and the dignity of the foundations. We called them "*chizzy-wags*," and had a particular scorn and hatred of their nasal tone in singing.

The under grammar-master was the Rev. Mr. Field.[1] He was a good-looking man, very gentlemanly, and always dressed at the neatest. I believe he once wrote a play. He had the reputation of being admired by the ladies. A man of a more handsome incompetence for his situation perhaps did not exist. He came late of a morning ; went away soon in the afternoon ; and used

[1] In Charles Lamb's "Christ's Hospital five-and-thirty Years ago," a very similar account is given of the Rev. Matthew Field, whose character is thus summarized : "[He] belonged to that class of modest divines who affect to mix in equal proportion the *gentleman*, the *scholar*, and the *Christian*; but, I know not how, the first ingredient is generally found to be the predominating dose in the composition."

to walk up and down, languidly bearing his cane, as if it were a lily, and hearing our eternal *Domi-nuses* and *As in præsenti's* with an air of ineffable endurance. Often he did not hear at all. It was a joke with us, when any of our friends came to the door, and we asked his permission to go to them, to address him with some preposterous ques‑ tion wide of the mark ; to which he used to assent. We would say, for instance, "Are you not a great fool, sir ?" or, "Isn't your daughter a pretty girl?" to which he would reply, "Yes, child." When he condescended to hit us with the cane, he made a face as if he were taking physic. Miss Field, an agreeable-looking girl, was one of the goddesses of the school ; as far above us as if she had lived on Olympus. Another was Miss Patrick, daughter of the lamp-manufacturer in Newgate Street. I do not remember her face so well, not seeing it so often ; but she abounded in admirers. I write the names of these ladies at full length, because there is nothing that should hinder their being pleased at having caused us so many agreeable visions. We used to identify them with the picture of Venus in Tooke's "Pantheon." . . .

The scald that I speak of, as confining me to bed,[1] was a bad one. I will give an account of it, because it furthers the elucidation of our school manners. I had then become a monitor, or one of the chiefs of a ward ; and was sitting before the fire one evening, after the boys had gone to bed, wrapped up in the perusal of the "Wonder-

[1] Which gave him an opportunity for a good deal of reading.—ED.

ful Magazine," and having in my ear at the same time the bubbling of a great pot, or rather cauldron, of water, containing what was by courtesy called a bread pudding ; being neither more nor less than a loaf or two of our bread, which, with a little sugar mashed up with it, was to serve for my supper. And there were eyes, not yet asleep, which would look at it out of their beds, and regard it as a lordly dish. From this dream of bliss I was roused up on the sudden by a great cry, and a horrible agony in my legs. A " boy," as a fag was called, wishing to get something from the other side of the fireplace, and not choosing either to go round behind the table, or to disturb the illustrious legs of the monitor, had endeavoured to get under them or between them, and so pulled the great handle of the pot after him. It was a frightful sensation. The whole of my being seemed collected in one fiery torment into my legs. Wood, the Grecian (afterwards Fellow of Pembroke, at Cambridge), who was in our ward, and who was always very kind to me (led, I believe, by my inclination for verses, in which he had a great name), came out of his study, and after helping me off with my stockings, which was a horrid operation, the stockings being very coarse, took me in his arms to the sick ward. I shall never forget the enchanting relief occasioned by the cold air, as it blew across the square of the sick ward. I lay there for several weeks, not allowed to move for some time ; and caustics became necessary before I got well. The getting well was delicious. I had no tasks—no master ; plenty of books to read ; and the nurse's daughter (*absit calumnia*) brought me tea and buttered toast, and encouraged me to play the flute. My playing consisted of a few tunes by rote ; my fellow-invalids (none of them in very desperate case) would have it rather than no playing at all ; so we used to play and tell stories, and go to sleep, thinking of the blessed sick holiday we should have to-morrow, and of the bowl of milk and bread for breakfast, which was alone worth being sick for. The sight of Mr. Long's probe was not so pleasant. We preferred seeing it in the hands of his pupil, Mr. Vincent, whose manners, quiet and mild, had double effect on a set of boys more or less jealous of the mixed humbleness and importance of their school. This was most likely the same Mr. Vincent who now (1828) lectures at St. Bartholomew's. He was dark, like a West Indian, and I used to think him handsome. Perhaps the nurse's daughter taught me to think so, for she was a considerable observer.

I was fifteen when I put off my band and blue skirts for a coat and neckcloth. I was then first Deputy Grecian, and I had the honour of going out of the school in the same rank, at the same age, and for the same reason, as my friend Charles Lamb. The reason was, that I hesitated in my speech. I did not stammer half so badly as I used ; and it is very seldom that I halt at a syllable now ; but it was understood that a Grecian was bound to deliver a public speech before he left school, and to go into the Church afterwards ; and as I could do neither of these things, a

Grecian I could not be. So I put on my coat and waistcoat, and, what was stranger, my hat; a very uncomfortable addition to my sensations. For eight years I had gone bareheaded; save now and then a few inches of pericranium, when the little cap, no larger than a crumpet, was stuck on one side, to the mystification of the old ladies in the streets. I then cared as little for the rains as I did for anything else. I had now a vague sense of worldly trouble, and of a great and serious change in my condition; besides which, I had to quit my old cloisters, and my playmates, and long habits of all sorts; so that what was a very happy moment to schoolboys in general, was to me one of the most painful of my life. I surprised my schoolfellows and the master with the melancholy of my tears. I took leave of my books, of my friends, of my seat in the grammar-school, of my good-hearted nurse and her daughter, of my bed, of the cloisters, and of the very pump out of which I had taken so many delicious draughts, as if I should never see them again, though I meant to come every day. The fatal hat was put on; my father was come to fetch me.

> We, hand in hand, with strange new steps and slow,
> Through Holborn took our meditative way.

## HIS JAILERS.

[" Lord Byron and his Contemporaries," 1828. " Autobiography," 1850.]

MY jailer's name was Ives. I was told he
was a very self-willed person, not the
more accommodating for being in a bad
state of health ; and that he called
everybody *Mister.* " In short," said one of the
tipstaves, " he is one as may be led, but he'll
never be *druv*."

The sight of the prison-gate and the high wall
was a dreary business. I thought of my horseback
and the downs of Brighton ;[1] but congratulated
myself, at all events, that I had come thither with
a good conscience. After waiting in the prison-
yard as long as if it had been the ante-room of a
minister, I was at length ushered into the presence
of the great man. He was in his parlour, which
was decently furnished, and had a basin of broth
before him, which he quitted on my appearance,
and rose with much solemnity to meet me. He
seemed about fifty years of age ; had a white
night-cap on, as if he was going to be hung, and a
great red face, which looked ready to burst with
blood. Indeed, he was not allowed by his physician to speak in a tone above a whisper. The first
thing he said was, " Mister, I'd ha' given a matter
of a hundred pounds, that you had not come to this
place—a hundred pounds !" The emphasis which

1 To which he had been ordered on account of his health
—ED.

he had laid on the word "hundred" was enormous.

I forget what I said. I endeavoured, as usual, to make the best of things ; but he recurred over and over again to the hundred pounds ; and said he wondered, for his part, what the Government meant by sending me there, for the prison was not a prison fit for a gentleman. He often repeated this opinion afterwards, adding, with a peculiar nod of his head, " And, Mister, they knows it."

I said, that if a gentleman deserved to be sent to prison, he ought not to be treated with a greater nicety than anyone else : upon which he corrected me, observing very properly (though, as the phrase is, it was one word for the gentleman and two for his own apartments), that a person who had been used to a better mode of living than "low people" was not treated with the same justice, if forced to lodge exactly as they did. I told him his observation was very true ; which gave him a favourable opinion of my understanding; for I had many occasions of remarking, that abstractedly considered he looked upon nobody whomsoever as his superior, speaking even of members of the royal family as persons whom he knew very well, and whom he estimated at no higher rate than became him. One Royal Duke had lunched in his parlour, and another he had laid under some polite obligation. " They knows me," said he, " very well, Mister ; and, Mister, I knows them." This concluding sentence he uttered with great particularity and precision.

He was not proof, however, against a Greek Pindar, which he happened to light upon one day

I.                                                                Q

among my books. Its unintelligible character gave him a notion that he had got somebody to deal with, who might really know something which he did not. Perhaps the gilt leaves and red morocco binding had their share in the magic. The upshot was, that he always showed himself anxious to appear well with me, as a clever fellow, treating me with great civility on all occasions but one, when I made him very angry by disappointing him in a money amount. The Pindar was a mystery that staggered him. I remember very well, that giving me a long account one day of something connected with his business, he happened to catch with his eye the shelf that contained it, and, whether he saw it or not, abruptly finished by observing, " But, Mister, you knows all these things as well as I do."

Upon the whole, my new acquaintance was as strange a person as I ever met with. A total want of education, together with a certain vulgar acuteness, conspired to render him insolent and pedantic. Disease sharpened his tendency to violent fits of passion, which threatened to suffocate him; and then in his intervals of better health he would issue forth, with his cock-up-nose and his hat on one side, as great a fop as a jockey. I remember his coming to my rooms, about the middle of my imprisonment, as if on purpose to insult over my ill health with the contrast of his own convalescence, putting his arms in a gay manner a-kimbo, and telling me I should never live to go out, whereas he was riding about as stout as ever, and had just been in the country. He died before I left prison.

The word *jail*, in deference to the way in which
it is sometimes spelt, he pronounced *gole*; and Mr.
Brougham he always spoke of as Mr. *Bruffam*.
He one day apologized for this mode of pro-
nunciation, or rather gave a specimen of vanity
and self-will, which will show the reader the
high notions a jailer may entertain of himself. "I find," said he, "that they calls him
*Broom*; but, Mister" (assuming a look from
which there was to be no appeal), "*I* calls him
*Bruffam!*" . . . .

On taking possession of my garret, I was treated
with a piece of delicacy, which I never should have
thought of finding in a prison. When I first entered its walls, I had been received by the under-
jailer, a man who seemed an epitome of all that
was forbidding in his office. He was short and
very thick, had a hook-nose, a great severe countenance, and a bunch of keys hanging on his
arm. A friend stopped short at sight of him,
and said, in a melancholy tone, "And this is the
jailer!"

Honest old *Cave!* thine outside would have
been unworthy of thee, if upon farther acquaintance
I had not found it a very hearty outside—ay, and
in my eyes, a very good-looking one, and as fit to
contain the milk of human kindness that was in
thee, as the husk of a cocoa. Was, did I say? I
hope it is in thee still; I hope thou art alive to read
this paper, and to perform, as usual, a hundred
kind offices, as exquisite in their way as they are
desirable and unlooked for. To finish at once the
character of this man,—I could never prevail on

him to accept any acknowledgment of his kindness, greater than a set of tea-things, and a piece or two of old furniture, which I could not well carry away.    I had, indeed, the pleasure of leaving him in possession of a room I had papered ; but this was a thing unexpected, and which neither of us had supposed could be done.    Had I been a prince, I would have forced on him a pension ; being a journalist, I made him accept an "Examiner" weekly, which he lived for some years to relish his Sunday pipe with.

This man, in the interval between my arrival and my introduction to the head-jailer, had found means to give me farther information respecting my condition, and to express the interest he took in it. I thought little of his offers at the time.    He behaved with the greatest air of deference to his principal ; moving as fast as his body would allow him, to execute his least intimation ; and holding the candle to him while he read, with an obsequious zeal.    But he had spoken to his wife about me, and his wife I found to be as great a curiosity as himself.    Both were more like the romantic jailers drawn in some of our modern plays, than real Horsemonger-lane palpabilities.    The wife, in her person, was as light and fragile as the husband was sturdy.    She had the nerves of a fine lady, and yet went through the most unpleasant duties with the patience of a martyr.    Her voice and look seemed to plead for a softness like their own, as if a loud reply would have shattered her.    Ill-health had made her a Methodist, but this did not hinder her sympathy with an invalid who was none, or her love for her husband who was as little of a saint as need be. Upon the whole, such an extraordinary couple, so apparently unsuitable, and yet so fitted for one another ; so apparently vulgar on one side, and yet so naturally delicate on both ; so misplaced in their situation, and yet for the good of others so admirably put there, I have never met with before or since.

It was the business of this woman to lock me up in my garret ; but she did it so softly the first night, that I knew nothing of the matter. The night following, I thought I heard a gentle tampering with the lock. I tried it, and found it fastened. She heard me as she was going down-stairs, and said the next day, "Ah, sir, I thought I should have turned the key so as for you not to hear it ; but I found you did." The whole conduct of this couple towards us, from first to last, was of a piece with this singular delicacy.

## MAIANO.

[" Lord Byron and his Contemporaries," 1828. "Autobiography," 1850.]

[AT Maiano] I passed a very disconsolate time ;[1] yet the greatest comfort I experienced in Italy was living in that neighbourhood, and thinking, as I went about, of Boccaccio. Boccaccio's father had

[1] After the break up of the "Liberal' and the death of Shélley, and when Hunt's health was poor.—Ed.

I.                                                      Q 2

a house at Maiano, supposed to have been situated at the Fiesolan extremity of the hamlet. That divine writer (whose sentiment outweighed his levity a hundredfold, as a fine face is oftener serious than it is merry) was so fond of the place, that he has not only laid the two scenes of the "Decameron" on each side of it, with the valley his company resorted to in the middle, but has made the two little streams that embrace Maiano, the Affrico and the Mensola, the hero and heroine of his "Nimphale Fiesolano." A lover and his vestal mistress are changed into them, after the fashion of Ovid. The scene of another of his works is on the banks of the Mugnone, a river a little distant ; and the "Decameron" is full of the neighbouring villages. Out of the windows of one side of our house we saw the turret of the Villa Gherardi, to which, according to his biographers, his "joyous company" resorted in the first instance. A house belonging to the Macchiavelli was nearer, a little to the left ; and farther to the left, among the blue hills, was the white village of Settignano, where Michael Angelo was born. The house is still remaining in possession of the family. From our windows on the other side we saw, close to us, the Fiesole of antiquity and of Milton, the site of the Boccaccio-house before mentioned still closer, the Valley of Ladies at our feet ; and we looked over towards the quarter of the Mugnone and of a house of Dante, and in the distance beheld the mountains of Pistoia. Lastly, from the terrace in front, Florence lay clear and cathedralled before us, with the scene of Redi's "Bacchus" rising on the other

side of it, and the Villa of Arcetri, illustrious for
Galileo.

But I stuck to my Boccaccio haunts, as to an old
home. I lived with the divine human being, with
his friends of the Falcon and the Basil, and
my own not unworthy melancholy; and went
about the flowering lanes and hills, solitary indeed,
and sick to the heart, but not unsustained. In
looking back to such periods of one's existence,
one is surprised to find how much they surpass
many seasons of mirth, and what a rich tone of
colour their very darkness assumes, as in some fine
old painting. My almost daily walk was to Fiesole,
through a path skirted with wild myrtle and cycla-
men; and I stopped at the cloister of the Doccia,
and sat on the pretty melancholy platform behind
it, reading or looking through the pines down to
Florence. In the Valley of Ladies I found some
English trees (trees, not vine and olive), and even
a meadow; and these, while I made them furnish
me with a bit of my old home in the north, did no
injury to the memory of Boccaccio, who is of
all countries, and finds his home wherever we
do ourselves, in love, in the grave, in a desert
island.

But I had other friends, too, not far off, English,
and of the right sort. My friend, Charles Armi-
tage Brown [Keats's friend, and the best commen-
tator on Shakespeare's Sonnets], occupied for a
time the little convent of St. Baldassare, near
Maiano, where he represented the body corporate
of the former possessors, with all the joviality of a
comfortable natural piety. The closet in his study,

where the church treasures had most likely been
kept, was filled with the humanities of modern
literature, not the less Christian for being a little
sceptical : and we had a zest in fancying that we
discoursed of love and wine in the apartments of
the Lady Abbess.    I remember I had the pleasure
of telling an Italian gentleman there the joke
attributed to the Reverend Mr. Sydney Smith,
about sitting next a man at table, who possessed a "seven-parson power;" and he understood it, and rolled with laughter, crying—
"Oh, ma bello ! ma bellissimo !"    There, too,
I had the pleasure of dining in company with
an English beauty (Mrs. W.), who appeared to be
such as Boccaccio might have admired, capable
both of mirth and gravity; and she had a child
with her that reflected her graces.    The appearance of one of these young English mothers among
Italian women is like domesticity among the passions.    It is a pity when you return to England,
that the generality of faces do not keep up the
charm.    You are then too apt to think, that an
Italian beauty among English women would look
like poetry among the sullens.

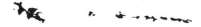

# THE RELIGION OF A LOVER OF TRUTH.

[From the manuscript, formerly in the possession of Mr. A. Ireland.]

### I.

I TAKE nothing for granted.

2. I make no compromise with the truth, because the compromise itself is a lie, and because it is by lies of this sort that schisms and quarrels are kept up, and men are perpetually seeking to defend wrong points instead of agreeing to find out right ones.

3. I assume nothing, as being wiser than others, or fancying that I have a right of any sort to keep them in a delusion. This is a principle of vanity, or of an idle despair greatly allied to it, and tends not only to make men hypocrites, but to maintain them in a belief that all clever men are so ; which is the worst thing for humanity that can possibly be.

4. I have nevertheless a strong, and I may add, in the largest use of the term, a pious sense both of the natural and the supernatural world ; that is, I am strongly sensible of the good that is in the world, greatly desirous to increase it, and can look with affectionate eyes into the great space and the other worlds about us, earnestly wishing that all which we suppose of good and beautiful may be true.

5. I believe in a spirit of good strongly and perpetually at work, though I know not how to define it, and I dare not give it a name that has been

so disputed and degraded by human passions. But I believe in [this] spirit, because of the good that I see and the yearnings for most that I feel.

6. I acknowledge the mixture of evil, because I see it also, but I do not believe in a malignant spirit or in malignity of any sort, because evil, I think, in the first place, is not always an evil as it is thought, and because all evil can be accounted for on principles, depending on circumstances and infirmity, quite distinct from anything like a principle of the love of all.

## ALIVE.

[From the manuscript, formerly in possession of Mr. A. Ireland.]

 ABANDON myself to you, my pen. Hitherto [you] have been under [my] guidance ; do you guide me now yourself, and be the master of your master.

The sultan, of thousand and one memory, applied to the fair Dinarzade[1] for amusement ; the giant Molinos to his ram ; entertain´ me in like manner, and tell me something I have not heard before. You may begin, as you please, at the middle or the end.

As for you, gentle readers, I give you notice, that I write for my own pleasure, not yours. You are surrounded by friends, mistresses, lovers. I am

---

[1] It was however the sister Scheherazade who related the tales.—Ed.

alone, and must contrive to entertain myself. Harlequin, in a like case, would have called upon Marcus Aurelius, a Roman emperor, to help him to go to sleep. The Queen of Golconda shall come to me, and help to keep me awake.

I was at an age, when faculties newly developed find another world about them ; when new sympathies unite us more closely with the beings around us ; when senses more awakened, and imagination on fire, impel us to seek the truest pleasure in the sweetest illusions : in short, I was fifteen, one day ;—when I found myself, at a distance from my tutor, galloping on a great English horse, with twenty hounds before me, and an old boar in the prospect.—Judge whether or not I was happy.

CHISWICK PRESS:—C. WHITTINGHAM AND CO.,
TOOKS COURT, CHANCERY LANE.

# ImThe Story.com

Personalized Classic Books in many genre's

Unique gift for kids, partners, friends, colleagues

Customize:

- Character Names
- Upload your own front/back cover images (optional)
- Inscribe a personal message/dedication on the
  inside page (optional)

Customize many titles Including
- Alice in Wonderland
- Romeo and Juliet
- The Wizard of Oz
- A Christmas Carol
- Dracula
- Dr. Jekyll & Mr. Hyde
- And more...

CPSIA information can be obtained
at www.ICGtesting.com
Printed in the USA
BVOW09s1955301017
499026BV00009B/207/P